ANGELS
OF
ABUNDANCE

ALSO BY DOREEN VIRTUE AND GRANT VIRTUE

Angels of Love (book; available January 2015)
Angel Words (book)
Angel Blessings Candle Kit (includes booklet, CD, journal, etc.)

ALSO BY DOREEN VIRTUE

Books/Calendar/Kit/Oracle Board

Living Pain-Free (with Robert Reeves; available November 2014)
Angel Lady (available November 2014)
Archangel Daily Messages 2015 Calendar (available September 2014)
The Big Book of Angel Tarot (with Radleigh Valentine; available July 2014)
Angel Dreams (with Melissa Virtue)
Angel Astrology 101 (with Yasmin Boland)
Angel Detox (with Robert Reeves)
Assertiveness for Earth Angels
How to Heal a Grieving Heart (with James Van Praagh)
The Essential Doreen Virtue Collection
The Miracles of Archangel Gabriel
Mermaids 101
Flower Therapy (with Robert Reeves)
Mary, Queen of Angels
Saved by an Angel
The Angel Therapy® Handbook
Archangels 101
The Healing Miracles of Archangel Raphael
The Art of Raw Living Food (with Jenny Ross)
Signs from Above (with Charles Virtue)
The Miracles of Archangel Michael
Angel Numbers 101
Solomon's Angels (a novel)

My Guardian Angel (with Amy Oscar)
Thank You, Angels! (children's book with Kristina Tracy)
Healing Words from the Angels
How to Hear Your Angels
Realms of the Earth Angels
Fairies 101
Daily Guidance from Your Angels
Divine Magic
How to Give an Angel Card Reading Kit
Angels 101
Angel Guidance Board
Goddesses & Angels
Crystal Therapy (with Judith Lukomski)
Connecting with Your Angels Kit (includes booklet, CD, journal, etc.)
Angel Medicine
The Crystal Children
Archangels & Ascended Masters
Earth Angels
Messages from Your Angels
Angel Visions II
Eating in the Light (with Becky Black, M.F.T., R.D.)
The Care and Feeding of Indigo Children
Healing with the Fairies
Angel Visions
Divine Prescriptions
Healing with the Angels
"I'd Change My Life If I Had More Time"
Divine Guidance
Chakra Clearing
Angel Therapy®
The Lightworker's Way
Constant Craving A–Z
Constant Craving
The Yo-Yo Diet Syndrome
Losing Your Pounds of Pain

Audio/CD Programmes

The Healing Miracles of Archangel Raphael (unabridged audio book)
Angel Therapy® Meditations
Archangels 101 (abridged audio book)
Solomon's Angels (unabridged audio book)
Fairies 101 (abridged audio book)
Goddesses & Angels (abridged audio book)
Angel Medicine (available as both 1- and 2-CD sets)
Angels among Us (with Michael Toms)
Messages from Your Angels (abridged audio book)
Past-Life Regression with the Angels
Divine Prescriptions
The Romance Angels
Connecting with Your Angels
Manifesting with the Angels
Karma Releasing
Healing Your Appetite, Healing Your Life
Healing with the Angels
Divine Guidance
Chakra Clearing

DVD Programme

How to Give an Angel Card Reading

Oracle Cards (divination cards and guidebook)

Angel Answers Oracle Cards (with Radleigh Valentine; available December 2014)
Past Life Oracle Cards (with Brian Weiss, M.D.; available October 2014)
Guardian Angel Tarot Cards (with Radleigh Valentine; available August 2014)
Cherub Angel Cards for Children
Talking to Heaven Mediumship Cards (with James Van Praagh)
Archangel Power Tarot Cards (with Radleigh Valentine)
Flower Therapy Oracle Cards (with Robert Reeves)
Indigo Angel Oracle Cards (with Charles Virtue)

ANGELS

OF

ABUNDANCE

Heaven's 11 Messages
to Help You Manifest
Every Form of Abundance

DOREEN VIRTUE AND GRANT VIRTUE

HAY HOUSE

Carlsbad, California • New York City • London • Sydney
Johannesburg • Vancouver • Hong Kong • New Delhi

First published and distributed in the United Kingdom by:
Hay House UK Ltd, Astley House, 33 Notting Hill Gate, London W11 3JQ
Tel: +44 (0)20 3675 2450; Fax: +44 (0)20 3675 2451
www.hayhouse.co.uk

Published and distributed in the United States of America by:
Hay House Inc., PO Box 5100, Carlsbad, CA 92018-5100
Tel: (1) 760 431 7695 or (800) 654 5126
Fax: (1) 760 431 6948 or (800) 650 5115
www.hayhouse.com

Published and distributed in Australia by:
Hay House Australia Ltd, 18/36 Ralph St, Alexandria NSW 2015
Tel: (61) 2 9669 4299; Fax: (61) 2 9669 4144
www.hayhouse.com.au

Published and distributed in the Republic of South Africa by:
Hay House SA (Pty) Ltd, PO Box 990, Witkoppen 2068
Tel/Fax: (27) 11 467 8904
www.hayhouse.co.za

Published and distributed in India by:
Hay House Publishers India, Muskaan Complex, Plot No.3, B-2,
Vasant Kunj, New Delhi 110 070
Tel: (91) 11 4176 1620; Fax: (91) 11 4176 1630
www.hayhouse.co.in

Distributed in Canada by:
Raincoast Books, 2440 Viking Way, Richmond, B.C. V6V 1N2
Tel: (1) 604 448 7100; Fax: (1) 604 270 7161; www.raincoast.com

A catalogue record for this book is available from the British Library.

ISBN: 978-1-78180-381-3
Previously published by CreateSpace (ISBN: 978-1-4609-4911-5).

Printed and bound by CPI Group (UK) Ltd, Croydon, CR0 4YY

TO GOD, THE DIVINE SOURCE
OF ABUNDANCE FOR EVERYONE

Contents

INTRODUCTION
TO THE ANGELS OF
ABUNDANCE

Abundance is our natural spiritual state of being, and we're constantly surrounded by Divine beings who want to protect and nurture us, and help us achieve our potential. These beings go by many names and serve various roles, but they're most commonly called *angels*.

Abundance really means a *feeling* of security and safety. Abundance has nothing to do with how much you have in the bank, or even how your finances are managed. After all, there are plenty of wealthy people who still worry about money.

Abundance simply means that you feel financially secure about your present and future life. That feeling of security is worth its weight in gold. And yes, of course, abundance includes the ability to easily pay your bills.

Abundance also refers to having plenty of time, ideas, confidence, love, and every other positive condition you can imagine. When you tap into the flow of abundance, it arrives in every color of the rainbow.

Our Creator made everything abundant, and is constantly creating new forms of abundance. Abundance is *so* natural that you have to take extraordinary measures to prevent its flow! In this book, you'll learn to identify and stop those sabotaging behaviors so that you can enjoy a flow of abundance that you can share with your loved ones and your favorite charities. You'll learn about the Divine contract that ensures you will be abundantly supported while you fulfill your life purpose.

You, like everyone, have a very important life purpose that only you can fulfill. It is a service that you agreed to perform in this lifetime to help others. Your purpose is a career or activity that you naturally enjoy and find fulfilling. It usually revolves around something you dream about, and admire in others in that field.

In our travels around the world, we've met thousands of talented individuals who dream of fulfilling their life purpose as a healer, artist, teacher, and so forth. They dream of helping children, the environment, women, or a cause that's dear to them.

Tragically, many people who would be devoting themselves to helpful causes find their time and energy diverted to jobs that are meaningless or toxic to them. They only keep these jobs to pay the bills.

Additionally, the wealth in the world seems to be disproportionately distributed. Unfortunately, some of the highly wealthy are using their financial power in ways that are hurtful to people, animals, and the environment.

We hold a vision of spiritually minded, ethical, and loving people manifesting enough wealth and worldly influence to invest in *helping* people, animals, and the environment. We envision people who are more concerned with leaving the world a better place than with personal gain.

Imagine having enough money to donate to charitable causes and to help your family. Imagine never again having to worry about money. Imagine feeling safe and secure financially. Well, you *can* manifest these imaginings into reality. Thousands of people have already done so, and you can, too!

We decided to write this book to share with you how you can manifest all of the support that you need in order to devote yourself to your life purpose. You don't need to suffer to make money! You can focus on giving of service, and still take care of your responsibilities. Whether you need more money; more time, confidence, ideas, connections, or opportunities; or some other resource, we will help you to tap into your natural abundance.

꙳ ꙳ ꙳

The term *Angels of Abundance* refers to the particular angels who ensure that our Divine mission here on Earth isn't hampered by lack. The angels know that we need material support to fulfill our life purpose, and they are able to help us with this support. *There's nothing wrong with asking Heaven to help us with finances and other material necessities so that we can devote ourselves to helping and healing others.*

The first time that I (Doreen) met the Angels of Abundance was when I was giving a reading for someone at a workshop in Colorado. The woman stood up and asked how to move forward with her life purpose. She complained that she had no time to begin the healing career that she dreamed of because all of her hours and energy were poured into a job that gave her no satisfaction and only paid the bills.

I immediately saw a cluster of angels around her who signaled that they were helping her specifically with unlocking her financial trap so that she could do healing work. These angels were very fast-moving and appeared to be detoxing her energy field from worries that exacerbated her woes. They reminded me of workers in an apple orchard, but instead of picking fruit, they were taking away clumps that appeared greasy and dirty. They explained that the clumps were the culmination of her continual worries and frustration energies. I knew they were specialists, and their name entered my mind as "Angels of Abundance," which I relayed to her.

Using pantomime and words I heard verbally and as thoughts, the Angels of Abundance told me that her financial trap stemmed from her overspending. She was seriously in credit-card debt, the angels told me, because she was trying to lessen her feelings of frustration through shopping sprees. The woman confirmed this as true. The Angels of Abundance continued with the message that the compulsive shopping was her attempt to fill an inner void and emptiness. This empty feeling arose from being unfulfilled because she wasn't working on her purpose. The sad and ironic cycle was that she had to continue working at her unfulfilling job in order to pay the bills that were triggered by her job being unfulfilling.

The woman started crying as she nodded in agreement. She, like everyone, had already heard her angels' messages. (We all do!) She knew that her shopping was out of control and that the interest payments on her credit cards were keeping her trapped kin an unfulfilling job.

She promised to seek debt-relief counseling and to cut up her extra credit cards to avoid the temptation to shop for unneeded items. She also heard her angels' guidance about healthful ways to fill her inner emptiness, such as prayer, meditation, time in nature, creative outlets, and conducting healing work part-time.

Since this reading, I've connected with the Angels of Abundance on behalf of many clients and students, and have learned their lessons, which are included in this book. I've seen the angels clearing away the energy clumps from financial worries and resentments. They look like greasy balls of oil, like something you'd find under a car. Not a pretty thing to have in your energy field, especially since they attract the very thing that you're worried about!

With the help of the Angels of Abundance, you can release these toxic energies and avoid financial worries. In addition to these specialized angels, you can also call upon these archangels for support:

- **Archangel Raphael,** the healing angel who supports our physical, emotional, and mental health so that we have enough energy to work on our life purpose. Archangel Raphael also guides and supports healers and would-be healers in their education and practices.

- **Archangel Michael,** who protects and clears us from the effects of fear and worry. Michael also knows the details of our life purpose and can give us specific guidance about the next step to take upon our path.

- **Archangel Metatron,** who helps us understand and work with the universal energies, including instant manifestation, and how to bend time in our favor.

- **Archangel Raziel,** who can clear away blocks and unconscious fears based in past-life memories.

- **Archangel Jophiel**, who helps elevate and beautify our thoughts so that we attract the most beautiful experiences.

This is a book about the lessons we've learned and the messages we've received from the Angels of Abundance. Now we want to teach *you* what the Angels of Abundance have taught *us*. Everyone can master and apply these techniques quickly.

All the information within this book is inherently known by each of us. We come to this planet with this knowledge but gradually forget it. However, not everyone forgets it at the same speed. The information can also be retained and relearned through meditation and disciplined prayer. In addition, nearly all of it can be acquired by watching children or by reading ancient texts in new ways. Some people would rather have the information presented simply and without dogma, and we will try our best to do so.

One very important fact that bears repeating is that all of us have the power within us to be as abundantly supported as we desire. Not one of us needs to be downtrodden and beset with poverty for a single day longer. We can all earn as much money as we could ever need, without having to sell our souls in the process. And we don't have to act in a devious or unethical manner to obtain wealth. In fact, acting in such a way ensures that whatever wealth is accumulated will *leave* the unethical person.

Some people in poverty-stricken cultures may never have the opportunity to learn this wisdom. Even if someone tried to teach them, they might not believe in the possibility of a better life. So, we are praying that as you use the principles in this book, you will share your newfound wealth with others who are less fortunate. In fact, sharing is a part of the lessons that the Angels of Abundance have emphasized, as you'll soon read.

Throughout this book, we use spiritual terms such as *God, Heaven,* the *Creator,* the *universe,* and the *Divine Spirit.* Feel free to modify these terms and use whatever is aligned with your personal or religious beliefs. After all, they all essentially mean the same thing: *love.*

 ༀ ༀ ༀ

Angels of Abundance is for those who want the freedom to leave toxic jobs, relationships, and other situations so that they can devote themselves to healing and helping work.

Finally, this book is especially for those who, upon first glancing at it for sale, thought, *That's too expensive!* By the time you complete this book, thoughts of lack and limitation should have left your consciousness and vocabulary.

We pray for many blessings on the journey you're about to undertake. The person you are as you read this Introduction won't be the same one reading the Afterword. You won't be able to finish this book without undergoing an epiphany that will give you the tools to truly manifest your desires. If you don't believe us, just read on. You'll find that you'll soon possess the confidence and knowledge needed to attain everything you yearn for—and more!

ASK FOR HELP

The first lesson from the Angels of Abundance is to *ask for help*. This may seem obvious, but if overlooked, this is the reason why so many people needlessly suffer. Unless you ask, no one—not even God—can help you. Because of the Law of Free Will, which respects your right to choose your life's path, God and the angels can't intervene without your permission. This means that you must *ask* for what you want.

Whatever help you need, God and the angels are always supportive. No undertaking is too great or too small for them to give you loving guidance and support. You simply need to turn to them for assistance.

Sometimes people ask us why they should talk to angels when God is easily accessible. The answer is: God and the angels are one, and there's no separation between them. The word *angels* means "messengers of God." Think of angels as thought-forms from the Creator. When you talk with and listen to God, you are sending and receiving angels. God is also *one* with you, Jesus, the saints, and everyone else.

Asking the angels for help can take many different forms, which are entirely dependent upon *you and your beliefs*. Angels are nondenominational, unlimited, and unconditionally loving. They are ministers, mediators, and messengers of God's will of peace. Angels can bend physical laws to help those who call upon them.

When I (Doreen) was writing my books *The Miracles of Archangel Michael* and *The Healing Miracles of Archangel Raphael,* I was very impressed by those who submitted their true miracle stories for publication. Each story was about a person in distress who had the presence of mind to call upon the angels in his or her hour of need. Whether fearing an illness, accident, attack, or invasion, these individuals stopped and prayed for help.

I admire these folks because it would have been so easy to scream or curse during these frightening situations. But instead of reacting out of fear, they had the composure to say (or call out loud) for Divine intervention. And because they asked for help, it was given.

Some people are afraid to ask for help because they don't feel like they deserve it. They feel they need to be saintlike and perfect to earn Heaven's aid. If this were true, *no one* would receive it! Help isn't a reward; it's an effect. Cause and effect means that you do something (the cause, which in this case is asking for help), and then the effect occurs (you *receive* help).

It doesn't matter *how* you ask for Heaven's help, but only that you *do* ask for it. You can call upon God, Jesus, saints, ascended masters, and the angels through traditional prayer; via meditation, affirmations, visualization, music, writing, or another creative activity; or by pouring out your honest feelings to Heaven in a heart-to-heart conversation.

Here's a sample of a prayer that you can say:

"Dear God and angels, I need help with [explain your situation]. *I feel* [express your honest feelings], *and ask that you help me and everyone involved. Thank you and amen."*

God already knows what you need, how you feel, and what you require help with. The reason why you're praying is to help yourself attain catharsis and release. When you air your feelings, you lessen their pent-up stress energy. It's like releasing air from a too-full balloon. Discussing your feelings gives you insights into the reasons for your upset, and can trigger epiphanies about solutions.

You must also pray because asking for help is required by the Law of Free Will. This is one of the Universal laws by which everything operates. We've been given free will to make choices so that we can learn and grow.

Your prayer could be formal and traditional, or free-flowing from your soul. You can speak your prayer aloud or think it (since Heaven can hear your thoughts). You can write the prayer as a letter to God and the angels. You could sing the prayer to Heaven. You could even, in a moment of frustration, scream the prayer.

Crystal Clear Intentions

Actually, those moments when you're angry are often the ones when prayers are instantly answered. The reason is that your frustration helps you funnel and focus on what you're asking for. The Angels of Abundance have taught us the importance of having "crystal clear intentions." This means knowing what you're seeking.

Manifestations are blocked when you keep changing your mind. Perhaps you're unsure of what will make you happy, or you wrestle with feelings of undeservingness. For some people, the issue is disbelief. They don't trust that their wishes could come true.

Let's discuss how to heal these barriers:

Feeling Unsure of What You Want

It's okay if you don't know the specifics to ask for. You can ask for a specific *feeling*. For example, you can ask to feel safe, financially secure, respected, fulfilled, and so forth. The conditions that yield these feelings will be guided by God's infinite wisdom, so you don't need to worry about the details.

Fear of Asking for the "Wrong" Thing

Our remedy for the above fear is to add this prayer to your request for help:

"This, or something better, God."

This prayer acknowledges that God's will has higher standards for you than you do for yourself. You may be willing to settle for less, but God—Who is your loving parent, with unlimited resources—wills your complete peace.

So ask for what you want, but leave a lot of room for God to upgrade your prayer. We've also had great experiences with praying for guidance about what to ask for. Ask for *anything* you need help with—including help with *asking* for help.

Fear That You Don't "Deserve" Help from Heaven

Sometimes this fear stems from organized religious teachings that promote fear and guilt. If you were raised to believe that only special or saintlike people gain "favors" from God, please spend time in prayer talking directly to God . . . and then make up your own mind. Direct connection with God is the birthright of all of us. God, being 100 percent love, unconditionally cherishes you. You don't have to earn God's love and help, as it is given freely to all of us, without any need to qualify for it.

Some folks belittle themselves because they have low self-esteem. They worry about bothering others, including God, with their problems. So they suffer alone in silence. Isn't it comforting to remember that God is omnipresent (everywhere, with everyone, simultaneously)? Doesn't it help to know that there's no possible way to "bother" God with your requests, because the Creator's infinite wisdom is omniscient (knows all)?

Fears of Being "Selfish"

If you were taught not to ask for anything for yourself, you may be reluctant to ask for Heaven's help. You can reframe the fear of being selfish by reminding yourself of how many people, animals, and issues you can benefit with your newfound abundance. The more you receive, the more you can give.

Your receiving doesn't take away from someone else. In spiritual truth, there really is an infinite supply of everything. *You* may be the one who helps with the equal distribution of wealth!

Disbelief

If you don't believe that your prayers will be answered, you may not say those prayers in the first place. Perhaps you were disappointed in the past when your requests didn't manifest. So you hedge against future disappointment by not asking at all.

You can heal this tendency by focusing on all of the times when your prayers *were* answered. Think about a situation when you were pleasantly surprised because you received what you asked for. Please don't allow the big disappointments to blot out all of the smaller miracles that have come your way.

Faith keeps us going through life's disappointments. It's important to keep our faith alive, even when it seems unwarranted.

Optimism is the positive energy that draws abundance and all good things to you. Without faith and optimism, you may miss the answer to your prayer! You increase your faith by asking Archangel Michael, the angel of courage and strength, to come into your dreams. When you're asleep, your ego is also asleep, so it can't override your Divine guidance.

As you're falling asleep, say this silently or aloud:

"Dear God and Archangel Michael, please enter my dreams tonight, and clear away any fears that have blocked my faith in the past. Please revive, renew, and refresh my faith so that I trust in you and my inner guidance. Amen."

How to Clarify Your Desires

Perhaps you fear asking for the wrong thing. Or it could be that you keep changing your mind about what you want.

Keep in mind that God already knows what you want, and knows what would be the "highest and best" for you. However, because of the Law of Free Will, you have to ask for help before it can be given.

Asking for help from Heaven is exactly like ordering a meal at a restaurant. If you ask for an avocado sandwich, that's what you'll get. But if you're unsure of what to order, you can ask, "What would you recommend?"

In the same way, you can close your eyes, take a deep breath, and say aloud or silently:

"Dear God, thank You for providing for all of my earthly needs. I ask that You continue to guide me clearly to everything that I need to fulfill my mission and to be able to provide a safe and healthful life for myself and my loved ones. Amen."

As you say this prayer, notice any thoughts, feelings, or visions . . . even if they're subtle. These impressions are answers to your prayer, in which you're shown and guided to what you need. They are the Heavenly equivalent of receiving recommendations of what to ask for.

If you didn't notice any impressions, you *will* once you're in a relaxed state, such as while meditating, being out in nature, getting a massage, falling asleep, or waking up. Every request is answered, although it sometimes takes a while for us to actually notice the response.

How Often Do You Ask?

You only need to ask once. You wouldn't follow a waiter into the kitchen while continually prompting him for your avocado sandwich. And you only need to ask Heaven once in order to enact the Law of Free Will.

It's not a problem if you ask *more* than once. You can do so as often as you want. The point is that it's not *necessary* to ask more than once.

However—and this is a big and major "however"—if you slip into doubts, fears, insecurities, and pessimism about your prayer being answered, be sure to ask for a renewal of faith.

Keep the Faith!

Faith is essential so that you don't block yourself from receiving what you've asked for. Otherwise, you may run out of the restaurant before your avocado sandwich is delivered!

"Please, God, help me to have faith, trust, hope, and optimism."

You can also ask Archangel Michael to enter your dreams as you're falling asleep. Remember that this is the nondenominational, unconditionally loving, and omnipresent angel who will help you release fear.

As you're falling asleep, say aloud or silently:

"Archangel Michael, I ask you to enter my dreams tonight and clear away anything that's keeping me from enjoying full faith."

When you're asleep, your ego doesn't push away Divine guidance, as it can do while you're awake.

Once you invite Archangel Michael into your dreams, he will lovingly and safely act like a chimney sweep who clears away anything toxic from your consciousness and emotions. You may even awaken during the process, and feel his detoxification.

In the morning, you'll feel shifted in a positive way. You may feel a bit tired from the process, but happily, your hope and faith will be renewed. And with faith, you can move forward confidently!

"Thank You, God, for . . ."

As stated before, it doesn't matter *how* you ask for Heavenly help, but only that you *do* ask. Studies show that prayers of all denominations have measurable positive effects. These studies have ruled out the "placebo effect" of positive thinking by demonstrating prayer's significant effect upon plants, infants, and animals.

Interestingly, it does appear from studies—and from our own field research—that "affirmative prayers" have a slight edge over "supplication prayers." Here's what those terms mean:

— *Supplication prayer* is when you cry out for help. You beg, plead, and request Heavenly assistance. Sometimes this form of prayer is said calmly, and sometimes with intensity. This form of prayer is especially effective when you're at the end of your rope and are very clear about what you need. Even saying the simple word *Help!* to Heaven will bring results.

— *Affirmative prayer* is when you thank God for the help that you're requesting. You express full faith that your prayers will be, and already have been, answered. You say, *"Thank You, God, for* [fill in the blank]."

The Power of Prayer

All types of prayer bring joy to the angels. As devoted and loving messengers of God, the angels rejoice in any attempt on our part to come closer to our Creator.

If you're in any way uncomfortable with prayer because of past experiences or associations, the angels strongly encourage you to restart this conversation with God now. Doing so on your own terms will achieve dynamic results, and also go a long way toward healing any residual pain you may be carrying. The power of prayer is limitless.

It's important to note that we do not pray directly to the angels, including the Angels of Abundance. That wouldn't make sense, because they are to God as our arms and mouths are to us: important pieces but not the whole. We don't worship angels.

If you're confused by the subject of this chapter, you're not alone. For so many people, prayer is considered a contingency plan for "emergency use only." Using prayer for something as mundane as asking for more money, a better job, or a promotion may seem petty to some and blasphemous to others. Fortunately, this isn't true.

Prayer is one of the most powerful methods of attaining anything in life. We were put here by a Divine being, along with everyone and everything else in existence. It stands to reason, then, that everything is within the reach of this Creator and can be bestowed upon us if we have the foresight to ask, and if it is in our best interests to obtain those items.

We do have free will, for better or worse. This means that while the Divine knows exactly what is best for us, it is not always free to intercede on our behalf. If, for some reason, the Divine decided to roll out the red carpet of abundance and luxury for us, what lessons would we learn, and how could we possibly grow? This doesn't mean that we must live a life of lack and suffering in order to learn, but we absolutely must learn to *ask* for the good things in our lives.

Asking can be done in a variety of manners. In some ways, hard work is a form of asking, as we're showing that we're willing to put effort into what we want. Each of us needs to take that first step in meeting the Divine halfway, and we must decide for ourselves which way is most comfortable and natural for us.

When we pray, we enter into a conversation with our Divine Source, and we're given the opportunity to allow a Higher Power to provide for our well-being. Just as good parents don't interfere in their children's social lives unless they're asked or there's danger involved, we must also ask for any help we want.

The method of prayer you use is completely up to you. You can pray to any Divine being of love and light that you resonate with. It can be a silent prayer, a simple prayer, a verbose and loud prayer, or a solemn candlelight hymn. You're free to choose whether or not to pray in the confines of a temple or church, your home, or the great outdoors. No matter how you choose to pray, the outcome will be exactly the same. Some organized religions have very specific precepts on how to pray, and if you choose to follow those, that's perfectly acceptable. Likewise, if you choose to buck convention and pray however you want to, that's just fine, too.

When you pray for abundance, it's less important to visualize what you want than you may think. The Divine knows *exactly* what you desire. Your mind is generally a very secure barrier, but when it comes to prayer, it may as well be an open book. For your own sake, you may want to continue visualizing the object you would like because it helps keep your mind focused (as explained further in upcoming chapters), but don't be too hard on yourself if you can't manage this every time.

It's possible to use prayer quite successfully in the absence of any other manifestation method. Since prayer is going straight to the Divine Source, it's the most powerful of all methods. However, because you're *asking* for assistance, sometimes the answer will still be no. With visualization and affirmation, there's never a question of whether it's going to work or not, only how quickly. For these reasons, using prayer alone is perfectly fine, but using a combination of all methods is recommended.

If you find that prayer is so effective that you don't want to bother with other methods, that's okay, too. You're the only one "keeping score," so no one will ever fault you for not using all of your tools, if you prefer one over another.

We've often heard that some people are afraid of "bothering" whatever deity they're praying to with their requests. This is never the case. Your Creator is anxiously waiting to help you, and any sort of communication from you is welcome at any time. The amount of love flowing forth from your Divine parent is nearly overwhelming, and the more you pray, the more you will feel loved. You will soon grow to feel very comforted and supported, and asking for help will become a natural thing to do.

Some people feel that they need to offer something in return for Divine assistance. Rest assured that this is in no way necessary. It's wonderful to perform kind acts and they'll make you feel great inside, but negotiation isn't a part of prayer. We don't want to dissuade you from doing charitable works if that's something you feel guided to do, of course, but don't let any perceived inability to perform those acts stop you from utilizing the power of prayer.

Prayer is the one method we use more than any other. That's not because we find prayer more effective, but because it's what we're most comfortable with. We have very close friends who aren't quite as comfortable with prayer, however, and they choose to use other methods with great results. Once we feel at peace with the method we're using, we'll have more success with it in general.

A typical abundance prayer I (Grant) use goes something like this:

"God, I desire to have the time to teach and write. I feel the need to have more money available to me so that I can focus more time on these projects rather than working for someone else. Please help me earn more money so that I can reach more people. Thank You."

That's a rather simple example, but one that's good enough to do the trick most of the time. Most important, it is sincere. You can make the prayer simpler, such as: *"Please help me obtain more money."*

Or, you can get very complicated. As mentioned above, the most important point is to be sincere in your prayer. When you really believe and have a genuine outpouring of faith, miracles can and do happen. If, however, you're merely "testing the waters" to see if this prayer thing actually works, then your results may not be quite so rewarding.

If, at any time, you feel uncomfortable using prayer to manifest abundance, then it's imperative that you stop. The only reason to use this method is because it rings true for you and you feel at peace. If that's not the case, you should absolutely not use this method and, instead, switch to others. Of the three main methods of manifestation—prayer, visualization, and affirmations—prayer generally causes more consternation among beginners, as considerable resources have been utilized to regulate its use within the confines of organized religion. While those practices and organizations have their place, they come at the cost of a bit of personal choice in some cases.

The power of prayer can be used for much more than simple financial abundance. In fact, this would be one of its more minor tasks. Although manifesting abundance is the primary focus of this book, when you've learned the practice of prayer and have achieved a degree of success with it, you may also notice that every area of your life starts to improve.

The first nonfinancial area where people start seeing an improvement is their health. Let's face it—your health is your wealth, so this is no small matter. In some ways, health improvements are the primary benefit of prayer, which has been successfully utilized along these lines for untold centuries. Recently, numerous studies have examined the efficacy of prayer in the medical field. The majority have found that prayer does, in fact, have an effect, even when the subjects don't know they're being prayed for, and the people praying don't know *whom* they're praying for. This is pretty exciting stuff.

These studies have also come up with some other interesting data, particularly in cases where prayer *hasn't* been effective. It may sound odd to be interested in the failure rate of a practice, but in this case, it has led to some positive developments. The primary cause of failure, or so the studies have concluded, is that the prayer was done without belief. An insincere prayer is generally just about as effective as no prayer at all. Some studies have shown that symptoms were *worse* when the prayer was insincere, but this data is probably skewed. It's highly unlikely that an energy force that responds well to loving prayer would punish an ill person because of the actions of another.

For this reason, if you're going to pray, keep an open mind about it, at the very least. Sincerity doesn't mean that you have to adopt certain religious beliefs or start praying regularly. It doesn't mean that you have to tell anyone what you're doing, and it certainly doesn't mean that you have to change your life if you're not guided to do so. All sincerity means is that you believe that you're honestly engaging in a conversation with a Higher Power, and trust that this power has the ability to help you.

Miracles of Abundance

When I (Doreen) was a young housewife with a limited income, I experienced miracles of abundance through affirmative prayer. One time when we were low on money and needed groceries, I said, *"Thank You, God, for the money to pay for food."* I looked down and there was a $100 bill at my feet! It was

Heaven-sent money. I went right to the market and bought my family meals, courtesy of God.

So many times, money appeared unexpectedly in response to affirmative prayer. I once handwrote a heartfelt letter to God, thanking the Creator for supplying enough money to allow me to pay my utility bills. I placed that letter faceup on a table near where I would pray and meditate. A week later, I received a refund check for the exact amount of my bills!

Another time, I wanted to buy a gift for a dear friend. I found a scarf that was perfect for her, one I knew she'd enjoy. But the shop only accepted cash, and I didn't have enough with me to pay for the scarf. I only had credit cards and checks, and the store wouldn't take either. So I held my purse and said, *"Thank You, God, that I have enough cash in my purse to buy my friend's gift right now."* Then I opened my wallet, and sure enough, there were two $20 bills, which I know I didn't have previously. I was able to buy my friend's scarf and get a valuable lesson in the power of faith and prayer!

We've met many people who've experienced miracles of abundance after they prayed for Heaven's help. Remember that it's only the love of money that the Bible warns us about. As long as you're asking to have your supplies met, and you're doing your part to work and be a good person, there's nothing wrong with asking for Heavenly help. It's literally manna from Heaven!

The beautiful Sermon on the Mount promises us that God supplies everyone's needs, and it's true! And the more you allow yourself to receive this bounty, the more you have available to share with others.

In Summary

The Law of Free Will is always in operation for everyone and everything. This law states that you have free will to make decisions for yourself. No one can interfere with your choices without your permission. But even though God already knows what you want and need, you must *ask* for Heavenly help before it can be given.

Always remember: It doesn't matter how you ask, but only that you *do*.

THE *HOW* IS UP TO GOD

A major block to abundance is worrying about how your prayers will be answered. All of your good work with prayers, visualization, and manifestation is like putting your foot on the gas pedal, and worrying is the equivalent of a brake pedal. So you go nowhere as a result.

A big cause of worry is the ego-mind (that part of us that's distrustful and afraid) trying to figure out "how" everything will work itself out. The ego-mind wants to know every detail about the way that abundance will come to us. The ego-mind wants iron-clad resolutions and assurances that everything's going to be okay.

This occurs because the ego wants complete control. Really, the ego is the foundation of all control issues. The ego is the opposite of faith. Since God is pure faith, and you were created in God's image and likeness, *you* are pure faith in spiritual truth. You aren't the ego, you aren't worried, and you don't have control issues in spiritual truth.

Yet, the ego can get very loud and pesky whenever it senses that it's losing control over you. The ego will try to talk you out of having faith that God will provide for you and your family.

You can get in touch with this dynamic right now by affirming:

> *"Thank You, God, for providing my family*
> *and me with your loving support."*

Now, notice how you *feel* immediately after saying or thinking that sentence. Does your stomach tighten? This indicates fear and worry. Or does your heart feel warm and happy? This indicates faith.

Next, notice *thoughts* that run through your mind. Do you have doubtful or worrisome thoughts? Are you trying to figure out a logical way for God to bring you more abundance? This indicates *fear.* Or do you feel like singing the praises of God for providing for us all? This indicates *faith.*

The Logic of the Illogical

Our ego-mind tries to problem-solve using logical scenarios. It wants to predict and control the outcome. So, it has you thinking, *What if this happens?* and *What if that happens?* Obsessive, worrisome thoughts preoccupy you, consuming your time and energy.

It's helpful to think about something wonderful and unexpected that happened in your life. Think about a time when you were pleasantly surprised. And think about the unforeseeable twists and turns that your life has taken so far. Could you have predicted all of the things that have happened in your life?

The truth is that your needs have always been provided for throughout your life. You're still alive, which is evidence that you and your life purpose are still needed in this world. As long as you're alive, you will have your needs filled . . . provided that you work as a fully functioning team member with Heaven.

This means that you'll be given Divine guidance to take action steps. You've got to be aware of this guidance and also follow it in order for your prayers to be answered.

Of course there are times when direct-intercession miracles occur (like the $100 bill found on the floor after I prayed for money to feed my family). But most of the time, you will be *co-creating* the positive results you seek.

The way that prayers are answered is beyond logical reasoning. Once you look back upon it, you realize that it *was* logical. It was also unforeseen. You couldn't have known the plot twists that would occur as your prayers were answered.

That's why we say that the "how" is up to God. God is mind. God is infinite intelligence. God is omnipresent. And God is omniscient. And your true self is one with God and God's mind.

Your true self never worries, because—like God—it knows only love, health, abundance, joy, and peace. So your true self can already see the solutions to any seeming problem you're presented with.

When you stay filled with faith, you can easily hear your Divine guidance. You'll know exactly what steps to take. But if you allow your ego-mind to cloud your thinking with worry, you won't easily hear the Divine guidance that is the answer to your prayers. Divine guidance is repetitive information that comes to you about action for you to take. Divine guidance can be:

- Thoughts and ideas
- Intuitive or gut feelings
- Signs from above

When you receive an idea, thought, feeling, or sign more than three times in a short time frame, it's most likely Divine guidance. Signs include something striking that you see or hear with your physical senses. Examples could be having the same book recommended to you three times. This is probably a sign to read that book.

Divine guidance will urge you to take positive and healthful action that will ultimately benefit you and your loved ones. Divine guidance also supports your life purpose, so it will help your clients and others who benefit from your mission.

Sometimes people complain that they feel blocked and don't notice any guidance. This usually means that the person is distracted by either stress, intoxicants, or fear. You can open your channels of receiving and understanding Divine guidance by avoiding intoxicants, and practicing stress-management activities such as prayer, daily physical exercise, eating an organic and unprocessed diet, spending time in nature, and meditation.

Of course, you don't need to practice a perfectly healthy lifestyle to hear the voice of God and the angels. Anything aligned with balanced living will help clear the static off the lines and improve your ability to receive Divine communication.

True vs. False Guidance

How do you know if you're really receiving true Divine guidance, or if you're just imagining it? How do you know that it isn't just wishful thinking—or worse, lower energies that are trying to trick you or steer you in the wrong direction? Perhaps you followed your guidance in the past and it didn't work out, so you lost trust in your intuition.

These are valid concerns, and not necessarily ego-driven fears. It's good to be cautious before embarking upon major life changes. So you'll want to notice these signs to ensure you're really hearing Heaven's messages.

Examples of Divine Guidance

After you pray for help, you will receive repetitive ideas, thoughts, feelings, visions, or signs guiding you to take action, such as an urge to:

- Make a phone call to a certain person or business
- Improve your diet or exercise
- Read a specific book or article
- Join a group
- Do research
- Take a class
- Write
- Take a trip
- Move to a new area
- Work on emotional healing

[. . . and so forth.]

Divine guidance always focuses on action steps to take now that will improve your future. It may not show you the whole picture about your future, but it will guide you step-by-step to the answer to your prayer.

All you have to do is be sure to *follow* each step!

EMBRACE THE MAGICAL MANIFESTATION POWER OF DESERVINGNESS

In addition to asking Heaven for help, you'll need to ask people to help you as well. If you're unaccustomed to asking for or accepting assistance, you're blocking yourself from receiving abundance.

The Angels of Abundance teach that giving and receiving are both equally sacred and important. The exhale matters just as much as the inhale. The tide goes in and out.

For those who are blocked in their manifestation, the usual issue is an unwillingness to receive.

For example, when others offer to help you, how do you react? How do you feel, and what do you do? Do you accept their offers? Or do you politely turn them down?

Do you worry that you're bothering others or making them feel unhappy if you ask for, or accept, their help?

Do you feel that others deserve happiness and success more than you do?

Do you worry that if you allow yourself to receive abundance then something bad will happen?

These fears all stem from feelings of *undeservingness*, which means feeling like you don't deserve to receive. If you feel undeserving, it doesn't matter how much you study and practice manifestation methods. Until you feel deserving, you will sabotage your success and happiness. You will push away all of the answers to your prayers because you don't feel prepared, ready, or deserving of them.

If this hits home and triggers emotions in you, take a moment to breathe, cry, and come to some realizations. This is the process of deep emotional healing that will allow you to accept help. By letting yourself see the truth, you will then be open to receiving abundance in all forms.

Abundance Role Models

We don't believe it's helpful to blame others for your financial circumstances. Blame is a lower energy, and manifestations occur more quickly when your energy (spiritually and physically) is kept high.

So we're going to look at your abundance role models through a learning—instead of a critical—perspective. A lot of your beliefs about abundance stem from what you learned growing up. So, please center yourself with a few breaths, quieting your mind and body. Notice the first answers that come to you as you read each question:

- *What do I remember my mother saying about money?*

- *What do I remember my father saying about money?*

- *Were there any other significant adults who modeled money attitudes and behaviors?*

- *What was their style of spending or saving money?*

- *How did the significant adults in my life talk about "the economy"?*

- *What was the energy of my parents when they would give me my allowance or lunch money?*
- *Did I earn money as a youth? How did that affect me?*
- *How were handled by my family?*
- *What stereotypes did I hear about rich people?*

These experiences influenced your beliefs about abundance. You may have been taught, either consciously or unconsciously, whether . . .

- . . . there's a lack of supply, or an abundance.
- . . . "the economy" affects your personal abundance.
- . . . you should blame others for your financial situation.
- . . . it's "safe" to accept presents from others.
- . . . it's a joy or a burden to give gifts to others.
- . . . you should trust good times to continue.

- . . . you're worthy of receiving good from others.

- . . . money is the root of all "evil."

- . . . money has germs all over it from everyone handling it.

- . . . rich people are "bad" or different from you.

Reading over these beliefs, your body will signal which are the healthier ways to think about money and abundance. Deep down, you know that money is like every other material object: a collection of molecules, made up of atoms. It is energy, just like you are! Money has become an agreed-upon method to trade goods and services. It has no inherent value (and don't get us started talking about the Federal Reserve or gold standard!) in and of itself.

Talking to Money

Your emotional reactions to money play a huge part in how much you receive, give, and have. In this next exercise, we will pinpoint any dysfunctional beliefs about money that could be blocking your flow of abundance.

This exercise will take about 15 minutes. Think of this time as an investment that pays huge dividends! Since we sometimes conduct this exercise at our workshops, you may have previously participated in it (or something similar with another teacher). This is an exercise—just like physical exercises at the gym—that needs regular repeating.

Here are the steps:

1. Hold a piece of paper money in your hand, of any denomination.

2. Take a moment to breathe and center yourself.

3. Focus upon the money in your hand, and remember that it's composed of energy, just like everything material.

4. Even though it may seem illogical, please try this: Say to the money (silently or aloud) as if you're having a conversation with someone, "Money, how do I really feel about you?"

5. Listen to the answer, which will appear within you as thoughts, feelings, or visions. Notice the first answer that comes to mind. Write it down if you'd like.

6. Next, ask the question: "Money, how do I treat you?" Notice the answer, which may surprise you.

7. Then, ask the question: "Money, how can I have more of you?" and again notice the answer.

8. Finally, ask: "What else would you like to tell me?" Notice and write down (only if you want to) all the answers, as well as your other thoughts and feelings.

Well? Did you have any realizations about limiting beliefs concerning money? Were you surprised?

In surveying audiences around the world after we conduct this exercise, we've found that people usually discover that they're:

- Disrespecting money by not seeing it as a representation of all the hard work they did (or a loved one did) to earn it

- Afraid of money, because they find it intimidating and don't understand the "rules" of making and managing it

- Feeling like an outsider, as if only other people get money

- Angry at money for evading them and for the harsh systems in the world that revolve around finances

- Chasing after money, but it's continually evading them

The energy of these attitudes pushes money away. Abundance is attracted to positive, loving, and inviting emotions. This includes having an abundance of love, time, ideas, confidence, motivation . . . and money.

Money is also attracted to the energy of respect. Respect the money that you already have by keeping it filed neatly in your wallet. Crumpled-up money signals that you don't really care about your finances.

Gratitude is magnetic in its power to draw abundance to you. One abundance secret is to write "Thank you" on every check you write. Send gratitude to everyone to whom you write a check, including the IRS and utility companies. Give thanks that you have plenty of money to cover these bills. Replace resentment with gratitude, and watch your bank account rise.

Overcoming Lack and Limitation

The more you affirm and give thanks that you already have abundance, the more unexpected windfalls you will receive. Even if there's no visible supply right now, and even if you have no idea how you're going to pay your bills, affirm abundance anyway. Say: *"Thank You, God, for supplying all of my needs easily and comfortably,"* and then follow any inner nudgings to take guided action.

Conversely, a block to abundance is the belief that there's only a finite amount of good. If you don't believe that you deserve good, you'll feel guilty accepting it, because you'll fear taking good away from someone else.

Infinite supply is the affirmation that there is plenty of abundance for all. Just because you have a nice house and safe car, this doesn't take a house and car away from someone else. The same holds true for every other need being supplied to you.

But what, you may ask, about homeless and impoverished people? They don't seem to have enough. How could there be infinite abundance with so many people financially struggling?

These observations are true. Yet, affirming poverty does nothing to help alleviate the suffering. Only helpful and guided action will suffice. You could become a wealthy philanthropist who donates money to the poor. Or you could get involved with a wonderful charity. Perhaps you'll teach others how to manifest fulfillment of their needs.

You Are Valuable!

Here's the truth: Money is neither good nor bad. It's a neutral object to which humans have imbued value and meaning. Humans have competed and killed for it. They've spent time away from their families in pursuit of it. But money, otherwise, is just paper and metal with an artificially assigned value.

Money's worth is your *time*. How much time does it take for you to earn the money you have? Valuing yourself helps you value the money that you earn.

You are very valuable! God created you with Divine love, wisdom, and intelligence. You have a much-needed life purpose that only you can fulfill.

No matter what you've done or not done in this life, you are valuable!

No matter what someone has told you, you are valuable!

You matter, and you are needed!
You deserve respect!

Releasing the Past

Undeservingness can also stem from past lifetimes where—as part of your role as a nun or monk—you took vows of poverty and self-denial. Unconsciously, these vows follow you forward in time to your present lifetime. They trigger suspicion of abundance in you, and wariness of anything more than meager sufficiency.

Even if you're unsure whether you took poverty vows, it's helpful to release them just the same. It can't hurt you to let go of old vows of suffering, and it may help you a lot.

To release these vows, go into a quiet space and say aloud or silently:

"Dear God, higher self, Jesus, and Archangels Michael and Raziel [whose name means 'the secrets of God'], *I am ready to release all self-destructive vows that I may have made in any other lifetime. I ask that you completely sever, undo, and untangle me from any vows of poverty, self-denial, or self-destruction. I ask*

*that all effects of these vows now and forevermore be undone
in all directions of time for everyone involved. Amen."*

You may feel shivers and chills as the karmic unzipping occurs. This is your DNA releasing old, stored-up energy, so that you can be free of the shackles that previously bound and blocked you.

ᕁ ᕁ ᕁ

In addition to vows, past-life cultural differences can affect your present-life abundance. In prior lifetimes, it was common to live in communal villages and monasteries where your food, beverages, clothing, and shelter were provided. Everyone worked and shared everything.

For many people, this is their first Western capitalistic lifetime in which they must provide for themselves. It's a difficult adjustment for those who spent lifetimes sharing as a team. In those lifetimes, there were no individual checking or savings accounts, taxes, or bills. So the thought of individual financial responsibilities can trigger negative reactions! And negative reactions block the flow of abundance.

It's helpful to realize that you're *still* in a communal setting in this life. After all, you have the ability to manifest abundance so that you can share with those in need. If you're not comfortable manifesting abundance for yourself, do it for the causes you believe in! You can become a saintlike philanthropist and give your money to worthy charities, or practice tithing in which you donate 10 percent of your earnings.

DEVELOP AN ABUNDANCE MIND-SET

Manifestation means that you acknowledge that everything and everyone is composed of the living energy of your Creator. Your body consists of the pure, loving and intelligent energy of God. So does your soul, your mind, and every other aspect that is *you*. Everything physical and nonphysical on Earth and in the universe also originates from this same energy. Therefore, everything is love, pure love.

Yes, there are painful and cruel situations that don't exemplify love. We are aware of the dark energy in the physical world.

But understanding both light *and* dark energy is the foundation of learning how to manifest.

In the physical world, there is *duality*, which means opposites. There is hot and cold, hard and soft, wet and dry, love and fear, health and illness, wealth and poverty, and so forth.

No Fighting or Chasing

Many of us who remember the non-dualistic world of Heaven waste a lot of time trying fight against the dualities of the physical world. So we push away debt, injury, fear, and so on. However, the Angels of Abundance teach us this important message: *Fighting against something means we are pushing against energy, which actually stirs it up so that it will disturb our otherwise peaceful lives.* This is similar to the old adage: "What you resist, persists."

So instead of getting angry or frustrated because of your financial situation, put your focus on the positive opposite. (We will discuss more of this soon.) In the meantime, though, notice the second part of this lesson from the angels: *Whatever you chase will run away from you.*

Chasing after money or anything means it will continually evade you. Nothing likes to be chased, as it's a frightening energy. Chasing after success, love, happiness, or money means that deep down, you're afraid it might not really happen. This fear drives you to "make" it happen, instead of trusting the loving energy to give it to you willingly. Chasing is a form of forcing something, and the universe resists force.

Chasing after money never works. Anything you chase runs away from you, because chasing implies that you have to force it to be with you. Chasing means you're afraid you won't get it without a conquering energy. *Fear energy in any form blocks abundance.*

God loves us, and like any loving parent, wants us to be happy, healthy, and abundantly cared for. God wills the same for every one of us! Those who live in poverty because they don't understand the energy makeup of the universe must be taken care of by those of us who *do* understand. When we prosper, we bring in more resources to help others.

The Economy Has Nothing to Do with You!

The ego is fixated upon externals because it lives by blaming others for its woes. One of the blocks to abundance is to blame others for, or worry about, "the economy."

In spiritual truth, there is no such thing as outside influences. There is only Divine mind, love, and spirit, which is 100 percent healthy and abundant—always. If you focus upon external things such as other people's spending habits, you will be influenced by the ego instead of by your higher self and Divine spirit. The ego is always about problems, lack, and scarcity. You don't want to be ruled by the ego at all!

Adam Smith, known as the father of modern economic theory, wrote about an influencing factor in economics called the "invisible hand." Smith and the neoclassical economists of today say that the marketplace always evens itself out as a result of consumer behavior.

If consumers believe there is not enough money, they will stop spending, and the overall economy suffers. But when there's a belief in abundance and consumers spend abundantly, the overall economy improves. This is also true on an individual basis. If you hoard money, fretting about every purchase and every penny, you will have an invisible-hand effect on your own personal finances and will never feel like there's enough money. And you will likely have money worries and fears that haunt you, no matter how much you have in the bank.

Every day, people go into business for themselves with new ideas and inventions and are extremely successful emotionally and financially. Each day, new people become successful, and they are no different from you.

If you point fingers at others and blame them for your lack of abundance, you've given your power away. Take back your power now and claim your authority over your own experiences!

Yes, there are many unfair and immoral elite people who are selfishly influencing world financial policy. Yes, the minimum wage is unlivable and corporations are buying political influence. But, you know what? You can rise above all of these realities, become extremely successful, and use your newfound money and influence to create positive changes in the world! Grumbling about the elite powers won't help you or anyone. But becoming a leader with integrity and ethics certainly will!

Don't Worry about "Competition"

Similar to releasing worries about the economy, it's also important not to fixate on "competition." The energy of competition is based upon the belief that one person wins and the other loses. Competition means that there's a limited supply, and not enough for everyone.

One reason why sensitive people are reluctant to manifest abundance is because they don't want to deny it to anyone else. There's an unconscious belief that if *you* win, someone else will lose. But if you really understand that there is plenty for us all, you won't worry anymore. When you can trust that money helps everyone—including your family, clients, and charitable organizations—you'll open the floodgates of abundance.

Steer Clear of Jealous Energy

No one is going to beat you to your life purpose, because no one but you can fulfill it. There's no race, and no competition. God doesn't play favorites. You have just as much love and support as everyone else. Promise!

Being jealous of another person's success says to the universe: "How come she has this and I don't?" All that the universe hears from that sentence is that you don't have what she has. And the universe delivers what you affirm and expect.

Similarly, stay far away from people who may be jealous of *your* success. They will consciously or unconsciously try to sabotage your progress. And never share your dreams with skeptics or resentful people who try to dissuade you from going forward. Jealous energy, whether it originates from you or someone else, is always toxic to abundance.

The angels always help you to manifest win-win situations. You win, others win. We all win!

Angel Words of Abundance

In our book *Angel Words,* we include many examples of how people improved their finances and other parts of their lives simply by changing the words they said. (We've included more abundance stories in this book's Appendix as well.) Here's an excerpt to help you with this important point:

I (Doreen) receive a lot of calls for help through my websites, radio show, and workshops. Frequently, I'm asked for angelically based answers to help resolve stressful financial and career situations. Invariably, I find that people—because of their stress—are using limiting words to describe their current situation. They're often unaware that they're using negative affirmations (such as "I'm broke") or that these statements are ensuring that their stressful condition will continue.

A woman named Carolyn Purchase has owned a metaphysical store in Nova Scotia for five years. In the past, whenever anyone would ask her how business was, she'd always reply, "I'll never be rich, but it pays its bills." Carolyn said that phrase countless times before realizing its impact.

One day she was chatting with a close friend about how the store should be a gold mine, since it's the only one in the region, with lots of customers and a great reputation. They wondered, then, why wasn't the store doing better? Why was it only making enough for Carolyn to buy inventory and pay the bills?

Carolyn got her answer when a customer asked how the store's business was doing. Just as she was about to give her standard, "I'll never be rich . . ." reply, she had an epiphany and said instead, "Fantastic! This place is a gold mine!" She said it with such conviction that she believed every word.

That was a year ago, and whenever anyone asks, "How's business?" Carolyn continues to say that it's fantastic and the place is a gold mine. In the last year, her sales have increased 40 percent over where they were the previous one . . . and they just keep climbing! All that has changed are Carolyn's words—from limiting ones to those with a positive energy vibration. Her words have *made* the gold mine.

The words that we say have a direct impact upon our finances, as Carolyn's story illustrates. And a woman named Livia Maris Jepsen went through a similar transition. A few years ago, Livia wondered why her prayers were only answered with "just enough," and never more. For instance, if she needed money to pay for something, she'd receive just the amount she required, and not a dime more. If she needed additional time to finish something, she'd get just enough time and complete things at the very last minute . . . and so on.

One day Livia visited a prosperous friend at the woman's mother's house. After serving her delicious meal, the mother asked, "Do you have enough?" and the friend answered, "Oh yes, Mom, I have plenty!" That was exactly what Livia needed to hear! She realized that she was always asking for and affirming "just enough."

Livia says, "If you ask the angels for just enough, that's exactly what you get. Try asking for 'plenty' and affirming 'plenty' and you'll always get much better than what you expect." Since changing her vocabulary, Livia is much more financially secure.

If asking for plenty of money creates discomfort, rest assured that you can use this extra cash for charitable contributions, helping your loved ones, and financing your Divine life purpose. Your increased flow allows you to give in even bigger ways!

Diana Mey is another woman who learned the power that words can have upon one's finances. Most of her life, she would say, "I don't have enough money for . . ." this or that. Diana's continual negative affirmations ensured that she'd never be able to afford anything she wanted.

Then Diana started seeing the numbers 818 repeatedly—on clocks, on license plates, in telephone numbers, and on receipts. She finally found the reason in my book *Angel Numbers 101,* which lists the meaning behind repetitive number sequences. The book explained that 818 was an angelic message to stay positive about money, and suggested that people who see this number use this affirmation: "I am financially secure now, and I have a surplus of money to spare and share."

Diana started saying this affirmation repeatedly, and today she is financially secure, with plenty to spare and share. She told me, "I now look at the world totally differently when it comes to money."

When I wrote a monthly column for a bookstore-owner trade magazine, I received many letters from people in dire financial situations. Invariably, they'd tell me that the city in which they had a bookstore wasn't a good place for a business. So I'd counsel them to please use positive words to describe the economy of their community (and the world in general). (After all, if someone says the economy is bad, what sort of effect do you suppose that has upon it?)

A woman named Lorraine Mills discovered that her negative affirmations about the city she lived in created negative effects on her business. When Lorraine moved to Japan from her native England, she kept saying that there wasn't a sufficient customer base in her new location to support her holistic therapy venture. Sure enough, Lorraine's business—which had thrived in the U.K.—slowed to a trickle. After several years of difficulties, Lorraine planned to return to England.

She made a business plan and visualized having a busy, full therapy practice when she returned to the U.K. Interestingly, though, that's when customers started coming to her practice in Japan! Lorraine realized that her negative affirmations about the economy of Japan had pushed away business. She told me, "I had affirmed there were no customers for my therapy practice in Japan, so that's what I got." When she visualized success, it was like rolling out a red carpet at her business's front door.

Sometimes, a painful situation will wake us up to the role that our vocabulary is playing, as a woman named Caryn Connolly discovered. After she was laid off from her engineering job, she started telling people, "I'm unemployed." Caryn desperately searched for a new job, without success. Then she realized that by continually saying that she was unemployed, she was *creating* that situation. So she stopped using that word, and shortly afterward, she was offered an engineering position that would pay all of her bills. Caryn said, "By changing the words I was using with myself and others, I was able to manifest abundance very quickly into my life."

Caryn didn't say positive words or affirmations. She simply *stopped* saying the negative affirmation "I am unemployed" . . . and everything changed.

Abundance Begins in the Mind First

With manifestation, you get exactly what you expect, every single time, without exception. There has never been a case in human history in which a person was rich, poor, or somewhere in between when that individual did not, at some point, *expect* him- or herself into that state of being. Sometimes we learn from our parents or culture to keep our expectations low, so we never ask for more. Abundance seems to be something that happens to other people.

To change your life for the better and banish the negative habits of your past forever requires changing the way you think and the way you speak. While you won't get into trouble for thinking or speaking negatively, you'll quickly realize that every time you do, it's a wasted opportunity. No situation on Earth can be improved upon by worrying or complaining, while nearly any situation can be improved upon by looking at it positively.

Why is this the case? Primarily because looking at a situation positively acknowledges that it has hope. That outlook allows you to think creatively to resolve an issue, instead of declaring the whole thing hopeless and giving up. Hope and faith are magically attractive energies that draw solutions, resolutions, and opportunities to them.

In practical terms, positive people are easier to spend time with than those we perceive to be complainers or excessively negative. It's human nature to help people who are taking active steps to improve their lives. Likewise, others are much more likely to help us when we're trying to look on the bright side of life. Beyond these practical implications, however, are the spiritual implications of our thoughts and words.

During the research and writing of our previous book, *Angel Words,* it became clear that both the words we say and how we say them contain a real energy. Positive words have a far greater energy than negative ones, and thus, have a far greater impact on the world around us. Every word that we utter leaves our mouths at over 700 miles per hour (the speed of sound). Crystal glass can actually be etched at the microscopic level by sounds, and it can only be assumed that all physical objects, being so closely related on an atomic level, react in a similar, if not identical, manner. Neuroscience has proven that our thoughts also contain energy, so it's not a great leap to suggest that positive thoughts are higher in energy than negative ones.

If we can, at least temporarily, accept all these energy concepts at face value, that says quite a lot about how we manifest what we really desire and not what we would rather avoid. Fortunately for us, positive words and thoughts are much more powerful than negative ones. Therefore, we can instantly negate any potentially nasty thing coming our way by turning it around and making it positive as soon as we recognize the negative thought or word.

Perhaps the easiest way to think of manifesting is to look upon it as a meal, in a metaphorical sense (like the avocado sandwich in the Message 1 chapter). The particular restaurant where you ordered this meal has the most extensive menu you could possibly imagine. Nearly any food conceived of by human beings is available on this menu. It sounds great, but the servers have no opinions of their own. You could order the most awful thing and they wouldn't blink. Likewise, you could order the specialty of the house and get a similar nonreaction from the waitstaff; their desire to simply serve you overrides any feelings or opinions. If you ordered an omelette when you actually wanted a sandwich, the assumption is that what you said is what you meant. So it is with our lives.

As such, specificity must become job number one when we're working to achieve a goal. We must not falter in our absolute conviction that we will succeed. While we do grow and learn each time we take a negative path, we must strive to discipline ourselves to the point where negative thinking is the exception, not the rule.

Nearly everyone is familiar with the phrase "Be careful what you wish for." Nowhere is this statement truer than when you're trying to manifest your desires, because you never know when you're going to get what you're thinking about. It could be good, it could be bad, but in any case, you never know when it's going to show up.

Most of the time, good things come into our lives; nevertheless, from time to time, we manage to put in that order for foul-tasting food, metaphorically, and it comes back to us. However, every single time we expect something good to come into our lives, it (or something better) comes to us.

Now this may seem surprising, because surely, at some point, you wished for something, and it didn't come to you. Why was this the case? A number of factors could have affected that particular wish. Perhaps you didn't want it as much as you really thought you did, so even though you *did* want it once, you changed your mind by the time it was coming your way. Maybe you simply lost hope or focus and, as they say, "gave up five minutes before the miracle." Most likely, whatever you wished for simply wouldn't have served a higher purpose in your life. Essentially, it wasn't good for you. Whatever may have happened, it's important not to think of that instance as the time you tried to manifest and failed. Even if you don't know why it didn't work, rest assured that there's a very good reason, nonetheless.

Remember that expectations are wishes. You could ask for something, but deep down not expect it to happen. You cancel wishes when you hold pessimistic thoughts about their viability. It's essential that you believe in the possibility of what you're asking for! If you ask for a raise and promotion at work, but deep down you doubt it will happen, your doubts are the wish that will block your progress.

Dwelling on why you didn't get what you wanted won't help you in any aspect of your life, let alone in manifesting true wealth. It's far more important to focus on the future in a bright and optimistic way. Keeping yourself in a positive state of mind helps ensure that you're only bringing into your life that which you truly want, not that which you fear.

Fear must be overcome precisely because we, as human beings, are so wonderful at bringing about what we think of most. Fortunately for us all, we're being looked after by Divine beings every minute of every day, and therefore do not have any real reason to be afraid.

Keeping that in mind at all times should allow you to forget all those things you'd rather not have in your life and let you focus on what serves you. When you're not feeling your best, or you feel a bit down about your situation, it's vital to keep track of your thoughts and words. It's when you're under the sway of particularly strong emotions that your thoughts and words manifest the quickest. At those times, you'll be most convinced of what you want, and are therefore the clearest in your desires—the key to an abundance mind-set.

HIGH ENERGY = FAST MANIFESTATION

If you need money (or anything else) in a hurry, you can speed up your manifestations by increasing your own energy levels. The faster and higher your vibrations, the quicker your thoughts manifest into physical form.

The Angels of Abundance taught us about the unfortunate Catch-22 that occurs all too often: A person is depressed about his or her life, and then everything else seems to become blocked. It's a "when it rains, it pours" situation!

To overcome this seeming "streak of bad luck," you have to take the first step. And that means increasing your energy levels so that you can connect directly with the fast-paced and high-vibrational energies of the universe. Now if you skip this step, it doesn't mean you'll be incapable of manifestation. It just means that your manifestations may come to you slower than you'd like.

In practical terms, increasing your energy levels means doing things that you may not feel like doing right now—things like exercising, detoxing, eating better, getting a good night's sleep, and so forth. You might think, *I can take better care of myself right after I have more money to feel more secure.* But that's backward!

Fortunately, the angels can help you. You can call upon Archangel Raphael, whose name means "God heals," to help you manifest motivation, time, money, child care, transportation, and any other form of support you need in order to take care of yourself.

Here's a prayer to help you increase your desire for healthful living:

> *"Dear God and Archangel Raphael, please help me to care about, and for, my physical body. I wish to feel well,*

and to have vitality and energy. Please release any fears I may have about living a balanced lifestyle. Please increase my motivation to exercise, eat healthfully, and take excellent care of my physical body. Thank you and amen."

Eating Well on a Budget

Many people say they'd eat better if they had more money. They'd buy organic items from the health-food store. Yet again, this type of thinking is *backward*. It really is an investment in everything—including your finances—to eat healthfully.

If you shop at farmers' markets, co-ops, local farms, or grow your own food, organic prices are comparable to pesticide-sprayed produce. Besides, with the health dangers of non-organic, you'll pay for eating the toxic chemicals in other ways.

Everyone should do their best to eat organic, non–genetically modified food as much as possible. You'll want to ensure that your fruits, vegetables, and grains are organic.

However, there's a myth that organic foods are too expensive for the average consumer's budget. While some organic markets do charge more than traditional stores, prices are leveling out as more consumers demand organic food choices. If your local market doesn't carry organic produce and other supplies, ask your manager to order them . . . and then be sure to *buy* the items to encourage the store to continue supplying them.

Farmers' markets, local farms, co-ops, and your own garden are the least expensive way to eat fruits and vegetables. Plus, you have the added ecological, community, and energy benefits of shopping and eating locally grown food!

Many families are replacing their lawns with homegrown food gardens. Think of the fun that you and your children could share by gardening and harvesting your own produce. You can easily grow food in planters on a balcony if you don't have a yard. There are also hydroponic and light-grown plants that require no soil or sunlight. *Everyone* can grow their own heirloom and organic foods!

Walking: Setting You Off in the Right Direction

In addition to eating healthfully, exercise greatly increases your energy levels. Not everyone is going to gleefully jump into a fitness program. Many regard exercising as a chore and painfully recall grueling high school physical education classes where they had to run ten laps around the schoolyard. Some will say, "Well, I'll try the rest of this book's suggestions, but I'll skip the exercise part." Others, who've been sedentary for six months or more, are wise to avoid diving into an aerobics-type program. Instead, they need to gradually incorporate exercise into their lifestyles.

Walking is a pain-free way to gently introduce exercise into your life and help you burn fat and calories. Although not an aerobic program (unless you walk briskly), it will start you in the right direction and perhaps inspire you to move on to a more intense workout.

This walking program involves adding three activities to your normal daily routine:

1. If you drive or ride in a car, always park your auto at the outer edge of the parking lot. If you take public transportation and it's safe and feasible, leave the train or bus one stop before your normal getting-off point. This will give you opportunities to walk to your destination, and it may also save your car from parking-lot dings.

2. Take the stairs instead of the elevator or escalator. You'll beat the crowds and will probably get to your destination faster than you would by waiting around for the elevator to arrive.

3. Once a day, go for a half-hour walk around the neighborhood or the area in which you work. Make this a firm rule for yourself, and always stick to it. After-dinner overeaters are wise to adopt the habit of getting out of the kitchen, out of the house, and outside into the fresh air. Homemakers, shift workers, and those who work out of their homes could take morning walks to get their metabolism going and inspire them to avoid overeating during the day. Others could take their walking shoes to work and go for a brisk walk during lunchtime. This is a natural way to burn calories and avoid the temptation to overeat during lunch.

Exercise, once incorporated into your lifestyle, has a ripple effect that creates an all-around healthy mind-set. After going to the time and trouble to exercise, you're not as apt to spoil your efforts with overeating.

If your schedule doesn't permit a walk because you get home late at night (or if you don't feel safe walking around your neighborhood), take a stroll at the local shopping center or mall. Just be sure to stay away from the dessert shops! Or, you could walk in place or use a treadmill on slow speed while watching your favorite television show.

What Kind of Exercise Do You Prefer?

Please don't make the mistake of waiting until you're in the mood to begin an exercise program, because that day may never come. Instead, push yourself to do something physical right now. If you don't belong to a gym, then maybe it's time to join one. Exercising at home alone requires a tremendous amount of self-discipline—something most of us don't have when we're first starting a diet and fitness program. Pick a gym where you feel comfortable, which is located close enough to your home or workplace so that you'll actually go there at least four times a week.

Many people are embarrassed to join a gym, thinking that they're too overweight to exercise in shorts in front of strangers. I understand this illogical logic, because I (Doreen) thought the same thing in years past. It's kind of like wanting to clean your home before the housekeeper arrives so she won't think you're a slob. However, don't fall into this trap now, because gyms are there to help you tone your muscles and lose your excess weight. Besides, I've found that most people working out at gyms—male and female—are too absorbed in their own worlds to notice those exercising around them. It's really important that you choose an activity that you enjoy, or it will be even more difficult to talk yourself into exercising.

Think about your natural tendencies when deciding what type of exercise to engage in:

— Do you prefer to be alone? Then you'll probably do best exercising at home. Since you won't have anyone around urging you to exercise, you'll have to schedule exercise into your lifestyle. You may want to do this by pairing another activity that is already an ingrained habit—say, your two o'clock soap opera or your four o'clock talk radio show—with the workout. This will trigger a reminder that it's time to watch your favorite program, or listen to your call-in show *and* hop on the Rebounder.

— Do you prefer to be with one other person? Then you may enjoy two-person sports such as tennis or racquetball. This may be an ideal situation as well if you and your exercise buddy make a pact to gently "bully" each other into working out on those days when you'd rather not.

— Do you like to be with a *lot* of other people? If so, then you'll probably like gyms and aerobics, yoga, martial arts, or dance classes. At these places, you'll have the opportunity to introduce yourself to new friends.

— Do you like to be indoors? Then choose exercises that take place in gyms, martial-arts studios, dance halls, or indoor tennis courts or swimming pools—or exercise at home.

— Do you prefer the outdoors? Then your activities would naturally be in line with tennis, bicycle riding, team sports, kayaking, jogging, hiking, or brisk walking.

— Do you want to lower your stress level? Then you'd be happiest with a mind/body/spirit fitness program such as yoga, tai chi, or rock climbing.

— Do you want to tone your muscles? Your ideal sport will involve weight workouts, such as free weights, weight equipment, yoga, jogging on sandy soil, or rubber-band classes.

There are other considerations to keep in mind—for example, your budget. Some exercise programs, such as tennis or gym memberships, can run into a great deal of money by the time you finish paying for gym outfits, workout shoes, and club dues. When I (Doreen) belonged to a gym, I was primarily using the elliptical machine and free weights. I found that it was less expensive to purchase my own elliptical machine and free weights and save the cost of the monthly club dues (plus avoid the lines that invariably formed to use the stair climber). Other workout programs, such as brisk walking or using an exercise video, cost practically nothing (although you should make sure to wear proper shoes no matter what exercise you choose).

Keep Yourself Motivated

How many times have you joined a gym, bought some home exercise equipment, or committed yourself to a jogging regime, only to abandon it a month later? If you're like most people, the answer's likely to be, "Too many times to remember."

Exercise, while such an important part of any fitness program, is usually the first thing to fall by the wayside when schedules get busy. For some, getting started is the hardest part, but then once these people get into a routine of exercising, they begin to enjoy it so much that they refuse to let it go. But for most of us, sticking with exercise is the hard part. We'll run, pump, or swim ourselves into shape and then stop exercising for one reason or another. And when we stop working out, we often return to overeating. This time, plan on sticking with your health routine!

Remember, there are no stopping points for exercising. We don't just get in shape one day and say, "Okay, that's enough exercise. I'm done with it forever." Here are some tips that will help you to stick with your exercise program. Try them out— they really do help!

— If you like the sport you've chosen, you're more likely to stick with it. Keep in mind that it may take time to find the activity that's right for you, so be patient if the one you're currently engaged in doesn't feel quite right. Instead of abandoning exercise entirely, switch to a different type.

— Schedule exercise into your day in the same way you would any important activity. Note in pen on your calendar which days you plan to exercise. Try to be realistic in scheduling your exercise time to avoid setting yourself up for frustration. Also, plan your exercise around your peak energy time (for example, if you're a "morning person," plan to exercise in the A.M. hours), and you'll feel more like working out.

— Don't look upon exercise as optional. Just as you wouldn't dream of missing that important meeting or doctor's appointment, keep your promise to yourself and exercise every time it's written on your calendar.

— If you begin to argue with yourself about why you don't have time to exercise, *stop*! Don't give yourself a chance to even consider not exercising. You don't argue with yourself about whether to shower every day, do you? Of course not! Do you ever say, "Well, I don't have time to brush my hair and my teeth"? No. Put exercise into this category of things you naturally do, such as dressing and grooming yourself.

— Buy a new exercise outfit or some new workout shoes. There's nothing like feeling attractive to give you the incentive to exercise. Just as you're probably more excited about going to work when dressed in a flattering new outfit, you'll feel more charged up about exercising if you know that you look your best.

— Reward yourself for exercising, but wait until after your workout to do so. For instance, you can withhold your evening snack until after you're done working out. Or put a dollar into a piggy bank every time you exercise, and spend it on yourself once a week or once a month.

— Pray for spiritual assistance in establishing your motivation to take good care of your body. God provides for *all* of our needs, including our emotional ones. However, we must remember to ask for help, as discussed in Message 1.

— Team sports can add fun to your exercise program as well as keep you motivated (there's nothing like a play-off schedule to force you to exercise). Call your local parks and recreation department or community college and ask about joining their volleyball, football, or softball team.

— Consider hiring a personal trainer. This person will help you construct a fitness routine to suit your goals and needs. Then the trainer will accompany you during your entire workout—either at home or at the gym—to make sure you complete each exercise safely and thoroughly. A smart friend of mine *prepaid* her personal trainer for three months of workouts. In that way, she ensured that she wouldn't quit exercising, as she'd done so many times in the past. Plus, she received a great cost reduction for prepaying. To find out the cost of a trainer (some even work on the barter system), call your local gym.

— Exercising with a friend is another way to keep your motivation high, have fun, and have someone to talk to while you work out. Make a pact with one another not to accept any excuses for not exercising, and you'll be able to push each other into sticking with a fitness routine.

— Form a walking club with your neighbors. Four or five of you walking together will provide lots of stimulating conversation, and you may feel safer walking in a group.

— Take your exercise program one day at a time. Set small goals for yourself, and be patient as you gradually increase your running distance, build aerobic stamina, or lift progressively more weight. Try not to compare yourself to others, except as a way to set future goals for yourself.

— No excuses (except illness or injury) are acceptable for missing your exercise routine. If, after being brutally honest with yourself about your reasons, you decide you really can't exercise in the morning as you planned, then reschedule your workout for the evening. Remember, excuses won't get your energy up to abundance-attracting levels.

— Some people drop out of exercise programs because they've overdone it and have experienced "exercise burnout." Be realistic when scheduling exercise into your life, and maintain a balance between too little and too much of a workout.

— Going away to a hotel for the weekend or for a business conference? Don't let your fitness routine be interrupted. This often breaks the pattern of exercising and may cause you to stop your fitness program altogether. Make your reservations only at hotels that feature workout rooms, jogging paths, gyms, or information on nearby health clubs with cooperative arrangements for hotel guests.

— Many people find that aerobic-type exercise sparks creative ideas. This has to do with the increased oxygen intake and serotonin production. For that reason, you might want to carry a small tape recorder or paper and pencil as you work out to capture your ideas as they occur. This will help reinforce the rewards of exercising.

— Finally, if your motivation to exercise is really low, try my 15-Minute Personal Pact. Tell yourself, "I'll exercise for 15 minutes. If after that time, I feel like stopping, I will stop. After all, 15 minutes of exercise is better than nothing." I can virtually guarantee you that after 15 minutes, you'll want to keep going.

Exercising regularly is as important as any of the other steps involved in increasing your energy levels, so please don't skip it. Remember: exercise isn't optional!

Angel Detox

The angels can help you detox from anything and everyone pulling your energy levels down. Remember that the *how* of making positive changes is up to God. Please don't worry about how you'll detox your life, as worry is one of the most toxic and energy-draining activities.

Think of your life as a hot-air balloon that seeks to go higher and higher. What dead weight needs to be thrown over the side of the balloon? What's the first answer that comes to mind? Trust that answer!

Ask God and the angels to give you the support to make positive life changes, but always remember that waiting to have more money to move forward is backward. *First* you make the positive changes, and *then* the abundance flows.

DO THE WORK!

Manifesting abundance means carrying your weight and doing your part as a team with Heaven. This is often referred to as *co-creation*.

It's not enough to sit and think positive thoughts. Yes, those positive thoughts will attract wonderful opportunities to you. But you still have to walk through the door of those wonderful opportunities.

We get so upset by spiritual books that teach that the secret to manifestation is to just hold positive thoughts. This sets people up for disappointment! They lose faith in positive thinking, because it doesn't work the way the book promised!

The real secret is that positive thinking is one ingredient in the recipe of manifestation. The others are outlined in this book. You wouldn't expect to bake a delicious cake with just flour as the only ingredient, yet that's what relying solely upon positive thinking is like.

This message from the Angels of Abundance refers to doing our part with human action steps. As an example: To write this book, we had to sit and physically type the words. The book did not magically manifest out of some cloud in Heaven. No matter how much we visualized the book being complete, and no matter how positive our thoughts, the pages wouldn't be here without the physical human steps involved in writing them. And writing meant that we had to say no to distractions and other activities. We also had to say no to any ego distractions that kept us from finishing.

Delay Tactics

The angels have taught us about the way the ego works to distract us from our life purpose. The angels call this process "delay tactics."

Delay tactics are any sort of behavior that takes up your time and energy so that you don't have enough left to focus on your true priorities. Delay tactics are usually behaviors that you engage in compulsively as a way of compensating for your fears. Common ones include:

- Overeating
- Substance abuse
- Addictive Internet surfing
- Compulsive shopping
- Worrying

Taking care of yourself includes devoting at least one hour per day, without exception, to focusing upon your passions, priorities, and purpose (which are usually one and the same).

That entails having the courage to face your addictions and other delay tactics. If your addiction is completely out of your control, seek professional help, including the online and in-person free support groups through Al-Anon and Alcoholics Anonymous. There are 12-step meetings for nearly every addiction, including eating disorders, compulsive spending, codependent relationships, and substance abuse. There are even wonderful and free-of-charge online 12-step meetings that you can easily find through an Internet search.

Many of these addictive behaviors are actually attempts to gain more happiness and peace. The ego tells you that if you have one more glass of alcohol, one more new dress, one more new relationship, one more cigarette, and on and on . . . then you'll finally be happy and at peace.

Be honest with yourself about how your particular delay tactic has accomplished the opposite, and has actually *interfered* with your happiness, health, and purpose. Have a conversation with your delay tactic and tell it good-bye. Be willing to forgive yourself and everyone involved in enabling your delay tactic.

Every experience you've ever had has been a teacher as well as an opportunity to learn and grow. So all of the delay tactics that you've been involved in have taught you something and have brought you blessings, even if you can't see them right now.

The purpose of delay tactics is to prevent you from moving forward. They represent your unconscious mind's and ego's way of preventing you from ever experiencing rejection or disappointment with respect to your dreams. Delay tactics allow your dreams to be perpetually in a state of suspension, where you'll never have to face the pain of having them not come true were you to go for them.

Taking Risks and Overcoming Fears

We procrastinate taking action steps because the ego says it's dangerous to go for our dreams. The ego says that we will fail, be ridiculed or rejected, and possibly lose everything and everyone.

But dreams, like lottery tickets, can only succeed if you take a chance on them. The truth is that every successful person had, and still has insecurities. No one enjoys failure or rejection!

And all successful people also had to take emotional, financial, and sometimes physical risks to make their dreams come true. A retailer has to risk money by opening up a new store. An author has to risk rejection and loss of time, with many hours spent writing and submitting material to publishers. An artist risks humiliation if others don't appreciate his artwork. And activists risk being labeled as conspiracy theorists, negative, or paranoid because they're speaking out about social issues.

Playing it safe in life gets you nowhere. Playing by the rules doesn't give you an *A+* in life. There's no one in the sky with a clipboard judging each of your actions.

Along the path of manifestation, there will be setbacks and moments that aren't fun. We have endured people ridiculing us and worse. Taking a public stance always opens you up to armchair critics.

But you know what? Every one of these experiences was a valuable life lesson. And it's the same for you. If someone criticizes you, it means that he or she has a lot of extra time on his or her hands to judge others. This is time that this person really should be devoting to his or her own life purpose, don't you think?

Each day devote at least one hour toward *realizing* your dream. It doesn't matter *what* you do, but only that you do something—anything—related to your dream . . . and abundance will follow.

VISUALIZE SUCCESS

The Angels of Abundance have a mission to bring peace to the world by eliminating stress about lack and limitations. These angels support our purpose by assisting us in visualizing our desires. They know that what we visualize, we will receive, so they gently remind us to always hold positive, loving images that we truly want to manifest. It is primarily for this reason that the angels encourage us to stay away from images and movies that depict negativity or violence. The angels want us to see things that bring us joy, not pain.

Fortunately, visualization is a remarkably simple thing to explain and practice. While visualization can be made into something complicated and unapproachable, we can assure you that it is, most likely, something you're already doing.

The Magic of Imagination

As we stated previously, we were all born with the magic of imagination; some of us have just forgotten how to use it. Consider the fact that children seem to have remarkable imaginations in comparison to adults. Is this because we gradually became enthralled by the "real world"? Or could we have forgotten, bit by bit, that our world is not the only "real" one in existence?

It is precisely when we forget or deny that magic exists that we constrict our experiences in our modern world. We can certainly understand the arguments that many put forward saying that they simply don't have time for such childish nonsense. Others will argue that the economy is the problem, or their family is blocking them. Although that may be true in the physical world, their lack of time has much more to do with being so enraptured by the "real world" that they can't fathom that another one exists. They also refuse to use the tools available to make sure that they do, in fact, have enough time.

Visualization is simply a method of calling up a picture in your mind. Yes, it's that simple. Picture what you had for breakfast this morning in as much detail as you can manage. Visualize the dishes you used and the utensils you ate with. Imagine the texture, flavor, and smell of the food. Can you really see that meal in your mind? Is it so real you can almost taste it?

Congratulations! That is visualization. Don't fret if you didn't manage to visualize very much detail with that exercise. This technique requires practice to perfect it. Practicing may take some work, but consider this to be training for your new job: that of manifesting your desires—not only at times when you find yourself wanting or needing something in particular, but every minute of every day. In truth, you're nearly always visualizing and manifesting, and you always have been.

Like any other skill, you can train yourself to improve your visualization abilities. One method to hone your skills is to stare at an object and then close your eyes and mentally picture it. Open your eyes and look at the object again, and then close them in succession until your inner vision matches your physical vision of the object. The more details you can mentally see, the better.

Please don't protest that you're "just not visual," because that's not true. Everyone has inherent visualization capabilities. In fact, the best way to become more polished with your visions is to affirm often, "I am very visual." Always affirm what you desire instead of complaining about what you don't seem to have. Affirmations attract, while complaints push your good away from you.

If, for any reason, you weren't happy with the level of detail in your visualization—or your ability to envision the mental picture you were trying to achieve—the time to work on this concern is *now*. This is one technique you'll want to have down pat before you proceed.

We understand that while the practice we described may be easy, it can also be time-consuming. It may also be a challenge to fit yet another thing into your already-busy schedule. However, consider these points when planning time to practice:

- **First**, you can practice this technique almost anywhere. Sure, visualizing while driving could be quite dangerous, but you can definitely try it during your lunch hour. You can engage in visualization practice while you're on hold on the telephone or watching television. You can also practice while you're lying in bed at night; it can even be quite relaxing and conducive to sleep.

- **Second**, the payoff for learning this technique can be quite extraordinary.

The reason we encourage you to practice your visualization so often is simple: If you're happy with the amount of detail you're getting, then it makes the technique that much easier for you. You don't want to be distracted by wishing that you were a better visualizer. In addition, the quality of the visualization really does have a lot to do with how well you manifest. Certainly, when you're trying to manifest highly specific things, you'll want a lot of detail. After all, if you know that you want a '58 Chevrolet Corvette, as opposed to a '57, your picture must be a lot more specific than most people's. Likewise, if you're manifesting a dream home or career, you need to achieve as specific a picture in your mind as possible.

On the other hand, "outlining" is a block to manifestation. Outlining means that you hand God a script for how to help you, and try to control the specific way in which your prayers are answered. Visualization means elevating your expectations, but don't involve yourself with worrying or trying to control *how* your manifestation will come to you. As long as it happens ethically and peacefully, it doesn't matter how your prayers are answered . . . as long as they are!

Additionally, sometimes our sights are set lower than Heaven's desires for us. Just like any loving parent, your Creator desires the best for you and everyone. We love this prayer, also mentioned in Message 1, which eliminates the worry about asking for the "wrong" thing:

"This, or something better, God."

Visualize with your feeling senses! In addition to seeing yourself as abundant, feel that sense in your body, too. Imagine the feeling of being completely secure. Focus upon that and ask Heaven to help you always feel that way. Remember that all prayers are answered, including your prayer to be safe and secure.

In our experience, most people seem to worry needlessly about doing something wrong. To be perfectly honest, the only thing a person can do wrong with respect to manifesting is to not try. When people forget that they have this power, they tend to slip into negativity and accidentally manifest all sorts of things that they would never actually want.

For example, think about what society often dubs a "worry-wart"—that is, a person who worries excessively or without cause. At some point in your life you've undoubtedly known someone who fits this description. The unfortunate thing for worrywarts is that, while they may have the very best of intentions, constant worrying can inadvertently attract some of the very things they fear. If they were cognizant of this fact, most people would avoid excessive worrying, almost without fail.

Tools of Visualization

Some people find the use of physical images to be immensely helpful. If you're a particularly visual person, you may find it useful to obtain a corkboard from your local office-supply store and tack up pictures of the things you're trying to manifest. Or you can create a "dream board" from a sheet of poster board, on which you glue images and words representing your desires.

These visual tools achieve two goals: (1) they help you remember what they look like with a great deal of accuracy, and (2) they remind you to remain focused on what you desire. When it comes to visualizing and manifestation, the best thing you can do is home in on something like a laser beam.

While you're visualizing what you desire or need, you're in the process of manifestation. It really can be that simple and effortless. The more you focus, the more you can fine-tune exactly what will come to you in your life. When we're talking about that tricky subject called luck, we're really speaking of manifestation. Does this mean you'll win the lottery if you manifest it? Maybe, but most likely not. Rather, we're discussing what people typically chalk up to randomness—for example, when they receive an unexpected refund from their utility company in the mail.

Believe it or not, this is exactly the type of thing that typically happens to people when they start to manifest abundance. Some get anonymous checks in the mail, or perhaps a gift from a long-lost relative, but the credit is applied all the same. Perhaps they get hired for a small side job at precisely the time when they need a bit of extra money. Of course, a person could manifest substantially more money than these token payments. Since this abundance is nothing more than a gift from the universe, the actual amount isn't limited in any real way.

So how does one achieve massive boosts through visualization? Simple: dream big!

If you want to be the CEO of a company, you don't apply for a job in the mail room; you apply for a high-level position. Sure, you may not get it, while the mail room would be a sure thing, but the chance of success is worth the risk. The same basic principle applies here as well. If you want to manifest a best-selling book, then the best place to start is to visualize yourself as a successful author. You need to really see yourself writing the book, finding a publisher, approving the cover design, and everything else that goes along with attaining that dream.

You also need to be particularly vigilant with respect to how you see yourself after the book is finished. Can you really picture yourself promoting it on television, writing articles, and going on book tours? Fantastic. If not, then you need to practice seeing these things in as detailed a fashion as possible. You'll use the same pattern of visualization, regardless of the dream you'd like to manifest. You really have to believe that it's the only possible outcome. You need to do this because you're putting an order in with the Universal Chef, and you don't want that order to come back to you wrong or incomplete. The bigger your dream, the more specificity is required.

The more you visualize, the easier it becomes. This may sound overly simplistic at first, especially before you've tried the techniques presented earlier in this chapter. It sounds almost *too* easy to sit and think of yourself in wonderful situations where there are no problems. You would be correct in assuming that it can be practically effortless. It's easier for some people than others, although everyone can get to the same level of expertise.

The actual practice of visualizing is so easy that everyone already does it every single day. What can take practice is bringing the visualizations up to the level of detail required to get exactly what you'd like. You're free, of course, to get by with "good enough" in your visualizations. To a degree, that's what everyone does. Since there will always be room for improvement, at some point you'll have to say that you're content with the level of detail achieved, then try in earnest to visualize and manifest something without it just being "practice."

When you're visualizing, it's important to remember that just because something can go wrong, it never *needs* to go wrong. Certainly, having a backup plan is never a bad thing, but your visualizations are always going to be best-case scenarios.

Of course, there are other people in this world with their own goals and ambitions, and some may not be as caring and nice as you are when it comes to competition. But those people really are their own problems, and you don't have to constantly think of contingencies. If their machinations come into conflict with the end result of your manifestations, just trust that they have their own karma, and release all negative thoughts and emotions about them to the universe. This business of manifestation is all about positivity, and you simply do not have time to think about or dwell on negative people and situations.

To give you a brief idea of exactly how powerful a tool visualization is, we will temporarily depart from the subject of manifesting abundance and go into the realm of health. Since these are closely connected areas of our lives, we hope you'll welcome a brief digression.

Grant: My wife's close friend, years back, was diagnosed with cancer. This can be a traumatic experience in itself, but as this lady was also a professional dancer, losing her physical health also meant losing her sole source of income. As great as dance companies may be, they're not known for providing their members with health insurance. Therefore, this good and talented person really couldn't afford to be sick.

Over the course of weeks and months, she gradually got worse and worse until her doctors had, essentially, told her to make sure that all her affairs were in order. Rather than give in to despair, she decided to change the course of her life and refuse to accept that she was going to die. She proceeded to see herself as completely healed. She could feel herself dancing, hear the crowd cheering, and visualize herself growing old. Her faith in this healing was so strong that she would never believe that any other alternative was possible.

As you can probably guess, she was completely healed of this allegedly terminal cancer not too long after. The cancer hasn't returned, nor is it likely to. Just because the doctors had given up on her didn't mean that she had to as well. The power of this healing was immense, not only in its scope, but also in its implications, including those for attracting abundance. The most remarkable thing about it was how utterly effortless it was. Through sheer faith and not a small bit of stubbornness, this woman was able to become a cancer-free person once again.

ᦕᦕ ᦕᦕ ᦕᦕ

Think of how much simpler the act of creating abundance in our lives is. If visualization and manifestation can do something so incredibly powerful, why would people ever think they would be unable to simply get a better job, get a raise, or start a business of their own?

The power of visualization is limited only by the belief of the person using the tool. If you can see something happening, it *can* happen. You can therefore see why, with an increased boost of imagination, your potential for manifestation increases as well. For this reason, any exercise to enhance your imagination should be pursued with all the seriousness of a university course.

Simple and pleasurable pursuits, such as reading fantasy and science-fiction novels or playing board and computer role-playing games, can be incredibly beneficial in encouraging imagination. Of course, as with all other things, it's important to use these tools in moderation. It wouldn't benefit anyone to spend every waking moment trapped inside a fantasy story. However, if used properly, books and games can help you develop a boundless sense of scope and wonder. This is precisely where you should be.

You may, at some point, be curious to see if it's possible to use the power of visualization for some negative purpose. After all, there are people who do not have the highest good of humanity in mind, and they could attempt to press any potential advantage, spiritual or physical. Fortunately for the rest of us, the answer is a very firm no. As we explained here and in our previous works, *Angel Blessings Candle Kit* and *Angel Words*, negative thoughts, words, and energies carry far less energy than positive ones. This means that while it's theoretically possible for someone to manifest something negative, it's far more likely that the force of the rest of us visualizing positive changes for the world would completely overpower the negative.

In *Angel Words*, we used graphics to demonstrate just how comparatively weak negativity is. It's vitally important to learn exactly how little power negativity has so that we're not afraid of it. When we give in to negativity, we increase its power and, ironically, turn it into something that we ought to fear. When we realize how little power negativity has in the first place, we can ignore it or scoff at it, limiting its power that much further. One simple daily prayer for peace, healing, and abundance for all is more than enough to counter whatever negative plots anyone may be hatching.

As contradictory as it may sound, it is indeed possible to spend too much time visualizing goals without spending enough time going about attaining them. As we stated earlier, the whole business of manifesting abundance is a Divine contract. This means that you have to hold up your end of the bargain.

Manifesting abundance can be made effortless by transforming things that you were doing anyway into something much more effective. However, you need to allow yourself to accept the incoming abundance by creating an avenue for it to come to you. You will need to have a job, your own business, or some creative project that you intend to sell for monetary gain. While it's very nice to have a private poetry journal or doodle on the back of napkins, it's unlikely that either of those activities will make you rich unless you first set out to ensure that your writings are read and your sketches are seen by the world. If, for any reason, you have qualms about your work, business ownership, or having the world judge your creative projects, you need to move through those blocks before you can continue.

MESSAGE 8

ALWAYS SAY POSITIVE AFFIRMATIONS

The Angels of Abundance love the use of affirmations. They teach us that any sort of positivity in our lives is such a beautiful thing, and saying positive words repeatedly is most beautiful of all. The Angels of Abundance encourage us to speak only loving and healing words at all times, but especially in our affirmations.

Like all angels, the Angels of Abundance are messengers. They hear our affirmations and relay them back to our Creator so that these desires can be granted. When we give the angels positive affirmations to deliver, they do so with much more enthusiasm and speed than they would if we only gave them negative ones. Throughout this chapter, keep in mind the sort of messages that you'd like to send, and try to avoid anything that would make *you,* as a messenger, cringe.

What Are Affirmations?

Affirmations can best be described as sayings that you tell yourself until you believe them. These sayings aren't false; they're quite true—however, sometimes they're not true *yet.* Their value is that they prepare your mind for success when sometimes—due to societal, familial, and personal influences—you're not ready to accept it. Another positive benefit of affirmations is that, like visualization, they help you define exactly what you'd like to attain—whether it's a beautiful home, a lavish vacation, a big raise, or even increased skills in automotive repair or interior design, for instance. Anything you'd like to obtain can, in part, be achieved by affirming it out loud to yourself and the universe.

A typical affirmation goes something like this: "I have a best-selling book and am a best-selling author." It can be as simple as that, and usually, the simpler the better. The basic formula of the affirmation requires that you use the present tense, for the most part. That's because your status as, for example, a best-selling author must be established *now*, not at some nebulous point in the future. If you're trying to achieve something on a specific date, it would be permissible to say, for example, "I am getting a large raise in one month's time." This would take into account your company's typical schedule of adjusting pay rates, and would be much more convincing to you than using the simple present tense ("I get").

In our first example, we used the affirmation "I have a best-selling book and am a best-selling author." The wording here is more precise than would appear at first glance. It could look redundant to someone looking at it from a purely logical frame of mind. However, upon closer examination, you will see that this is actually two affirmations in one. The first is that the book you're attempting to sell is a bestseller. That's great news and something to be proud of. The second is that *you* are a best-selling author. This would imply that *all* of the books you intend to sell will be bestsellers. You can see why this double affirmation would be much more powerful than simply stating, "I have a best-selling book." We are going for massive abundance here!

By the same token, you could say, "I have sold my first painting. I am a popular, professional artist." This would achieve much the same effect for those in the art field. For someone who's gainfully employed, a similarly effective affirmation would go something like this: "I am getting a large raise in one month's time. I am a valued employee." Of course, this two-prong method isn't required, and there's absolutely nothing wronged with stating only one affirmation at a time. We've simply found the double-affirmation technique to be far more effective in the long run. Try both methods and use the one that feels best to you.

You'll want to repeat your affirmation a number of times throughout the day. Some people start saying theirs when they're getting ready to go to bed. In many circles, the nightly affirmation has replaced the bedtime prayer. The repetition is important because, as marketing folks so often tell us, it takes several tries before our brains really absorb a message. However, once it *is* absorbed, it tends to stay that way.

How long, exactly, will you be expected to repeat these affirmations? Fortunately, they do come with an expiration date. In the example, "I have a best-selling book and am a best-selling author," it would bear repeating until the stated fact is firmly established as truth. When your first and second bestsellers are on the market, you can pretty much assume that your affirmation has "taken." Of course, you're not under any obligation to stop saying the affirmation at that point. Indeed, quitting a winning strategy might be of dubious merit, but you can at least be assured that you can stop once you've achieved your goal.

If you've been using the affirmation "I am getting a large raise in one month's time," and at the end of that month, you do indeed get that large raise, why not keep it up? If your company doesn't do pay-rate adjustments every month, it would be a minor modification of your established affirmation to take into account the next pay-adjustment period. Since this technique is designed to benefit you, you're free to start and stop at any time, without fear of reproach or judgment by anyone else.

Affirmations aren't limited to simple abundance sayings. Anything you'd like to do can be made easier, better, and faster by using affirmations. You could even, for example, say an affirmation that increases the yield of your vegetable garden. Saying "My vegetable garden is highly productive, and I am a wise and knowledgeable gardener" can and will produce some fantastic results. Along those lines, you can create an affirmation to support anything you want.

Affirmations + Visualization

You might have already guessed how affirmations and visualization work together. Your success with visualization depends entirely on your imagination, and through visualization, you can increase the *power* of your imagination. Likewise, your affirmations depend on your visualizations. Before you can come up with an affirmation, you must know what you're trying to achieve. The best way to determine that is to visualize it in detail.

Conversely, it's possible and highly likely that by using your affirmations regularly, you'll even be able to visualize your goal with heightened clarity. Constant repetition of affirmations gets the brain used to the idea of the desired goal. The more familiar you are with this goal, the better able you are to visualize it as a reality. The more you affirm, the better your visualizations will be, and the more you visualize, the more effective your affirmations will be!

Affirmations can be performed anywhere (although in public, you may be accused of talking to yourself). Our brains are also remarkable in that they can multitask in amazing ways. There are very few activities that saying affirmations interferes with. Likewise, there are very few jobs where performing affirmations is inappropriate. Some other employees, including the higher-ups, may use them as well. This is particularly true in sales fields and on sports teams.

While affirmations may seem "out there" to some of the uninitiated at your office, in our capitalist society, we value results far above skepticism and propriety. If your sales figures are even one percent higher as a result of your affirmations, we can almost guarantee that your co-workers and employers will be open to the use of these remarkable tools.

Obviously, a one percent increase in anything isn't all that much, but it does illustrate how small a margin it takes for someone to go from a disbeliever to a practitioner. Imagine, then, how much more seriously your co-workers will take you when you start achieving a 5 percent or more increase in your income. Of course, this is just an example, as not everyone is in a sales position. But regardless of how you measure your success in the workplace, it can be enhanced through the use of affirmations.

ᕯ ᕯ ᕯ

While you read this chapter, try this simple affirmation: "I am capable and deserving of achieving all that is described and more." Periodically, repeat this to yourself and see how quickly you attain results. You'll know you've had a positive result when some form of unexpected abundance comes your way. Obviously, this can take drastically different forms depending on the individual person, but *you* should be able to recognize it when it comes. As for how much time it takes, that is up to the universe, but generally, the results can come incredibly fast.

In some ways, affirmations work like advertising. That is, you do the affirmation now, and the payoff comes later. This can lead to a "lag time" in which it could seem that nothing is happening. Once you're over this hurdle, you'll see nearly constant results of your past efforts. If you stop at this point, you'll still see the effects for a time until the abundance "catches up" with the affirmations you've already tried.

Stopping is an easy mistake to make, because it appears that we can be complacent and still reap the benefits of our affirmations. For this reason, we encourage you to keep the "lag time" in mind.

When discussing these techniques with skeptics and the un-initiated, it does help to remind them that the act of affirmation does not contradict any religious practice. It's an entirely non-denominational act, which will not require people to renounce or affirm a belief in any organization or faith. They certainly won't be punished for trying these techniques. On the contrary, they'll be able to reap rewards for their efforts.

The theological considerations behind these rewards can vary dramatically between different people and belief structures. For the most part, we recommend avoiding that area, as it's highly subjective. You can, of course, choose to enter into a debate, but it's far better to go into a discussion of that sort armed with the awareness that no one person will ever know all there is to know about Divine intervention. How it works and why it works are topics for the grand theological societies and universities to tackle; it is sufficient to know, for our purposes, that it *does* work.

Types of Affirmations

Affirmations can generally be placed in one of the following three categories:

1. Constant affirmations

2. Acquisition affirmations

3. Emergency affirmations

Obviously, from time to time, you'll find affirmations that don't fit into any of these categories, but for the purposes of this chapter, we will focus primarily on these three.

— The first category is called **constant affirmations**, because these are the ones that a person repeats on a regular basis. "I am an effective manager," and "I have an excellent sales record" are both examples of this category. This type of affirmation is particularly useful for maintaining or gradually increasing the level of productivity or abundance in your life. By regularly repeating such positive phrases, you're training your brain—and informing the universe—that this really is what you want and the minimum you're willing to accept. These phrases wouldn't fit into the other two categories because they don't address a specific or urgent need. Affirmations that fall under the "constant affirmations" heading are generally expressed for much of a person's life, or at least throughout his or her working career.

You can use constant affirmations to maintain or benefit other areas of your life, too. It would be perfectly acceptable and effective to state: "I am a great father," or "My family life is peaceful, harmonious, and fulfilling for us all." If any area of your life presents consistent challenges, you can use this category of affirmations to fix those as well. The next time you're stressed about your drive to work, try saying something along the lines of: "My commute to work is perfectly uncongested, safe, and stress-free." Some people may find constant affirmations to be a bit tedious or unfulfilling, but since this isn't the type of affirmation typically used to enact sweeping and radical changes in a very short period of time, it's particularly important to be patient here.

Often, this category can yield dramatic results, but over a much longer timeline than some people would prefer. Also keep in mind that they're called "constant" for a very good reason— these are sayings that you'll want to repeat for the foreseeable future. There's no built-in expiration date because who can really quantify what an effective manager or great dad really is? These are certainly understandable complaints, but the long-term benefits of this classification of affirmation cannot be denied. It's in your best interests to start a constant affirmation and stick to it throughout your life. It is undeniably a task that requires discipline, and that can only lead to further financial gain.

There are times when a constant affirmation isn't the right choice. When you need something done—and done now— you'll be much better served with other methods. Certainly, you're free to try constant affirmations, but the results may not be as dramatic or immediate as you desire. It would be nice if one type of affirmation could apply in every instance, but that, sadly, is just not the case. With practice, you will instinctively know when to use the constant affirmation and when to switch to something more immediate.

— The second classification of affirmation is called the **acquisition affirmation.** These affirmations are used, as the name implies, to acquire specific things in your life. *Anything* that you desire will become yours with thoughtful application of this affirmation. You may be thinking, *Did I read that right? Surely they can't mean anything.*

The answer is, yes, you did read that right, and you can absolutely acquire any physical object that you desire. Certainly, there are limitations when it comes to people. Sometimes people desire other people, but regardless of what they do, those other people won't reciprocate. That cannot be fixed with this method or with any other method that any sane person would use. However, any tangible, nonsentient object is within your grasp.

This principle is loosely based on the fact that every object, including you, is made up of microscopic atoms, which, at their very core, are magnetically charged. This affirmation allows you to change the charge within yourself so it becomes the polar opposite of another object's, thereby attracting it like a magnet. If this sounds needlessly esoteric, you're free to ignore the reason this principle works or even supply an answer that satisfies you more. The fact that it *does* work is undeniable.

A simple acquisition affirmation could go something like this: "I have $1 million in my bank account," or "I have a brand-new electric car." Again, it's important to speak in the present tense with these affirmations. You're stating that you're in possession of this item now, not in some indeterminate future. It helps to be very clear on what you want. If you say, "I have a lot of money," or "I have a car," what does that really mean? A lot of money to you could be a trifling sum to others, and vice versa. Likewise, a car can be anything from a Bentley to a beat-up old Buick. In the realm of abundance, specificity is king.

These types of affirmations don't have any sort of built-in timeline. You can try to establish an artificial timeline, along the lines of: "I will have a brand-new car within two weeks." However, that manipulation of the sentence construction violates one of the principal laws of affirmations—to say them in the present tense. You're free to try out this little trick, and no harm will come to you by doing so, but you may be disappointed by the results if you're holding on to too many expectations concerning the timeline. Patience is an incredibly valuable virtue to possess when it comes to manifesting—in all of its guises.

When we let go and simply allow nature to take its course, then the most powerful magic occurs. Forcing things into place isn't an organic process and will ultimately lead to nothing. We must cultivate in ourselves a natural timeline and let things come to us as they're needed, while being open to them when they do come.

Acquisition affirmations are particularly powerful when seeking a new job or position. While the constant affirmation is terrific for maintaining and gradually improving a career, the acquisition affirmation is the "go-to guy" for dramatic upward progression. If you feel that you've languished too long in a position that's far below your skill set, then the acquisition affirmation will allow you to attain upward mobility without any risk of appearing too ambitious or ungrateful for what you currently have. Using this technique, you may entertain job offers from competitors or have a promotion spontaneously bestowed upon you.

If you're competing for a position that you feel you truly deserve more than anyone else does, and you know when the decision is going to be made, the acquisition affirmation isn't the best choice. Again, this affirmation category has no time limit or expiration date. What you're manifesting will come to you, but the date isn't certain. You can be assured that it will occur at the best time imaginable for you, the universe, and the object in question, but no one can ever tell you exactly when that's likely to happen.

— The third classification of affirmation is called the **emergency affirmation.** The term *emergency* refers to the need for timeliness, rather than implying that someone is in danger of some sort. However, if anyone *were* faced with danger, this would certainly be the affirmation to use. It would also be the right one if, as in the previous example, you were attempting to gain recognition for a promotion that's happening on a specific schedule. These affirmations are unique in that they *do* have a time limit and expiration date.

A simple emergency affirmation would look something like this: "I am safe and surrounded by love now," or "I am promoted at my job review next Tuesday." As with the previous classes of affirmations, it's important to use the present tense or specify an exact date. Using words such as *someday* or *soon* is a good way to go nowhere fast, because no one knows when "someday" and "soon" will really occur.

Do you remember when you were a kid and asked whether you could do something and received a "maybe" or "soon" in response? It was probably pretty frustrating and may have left you feeling a bit confused and unfulfilled. That is an instinctual response to the ambiguity of those words. You naturally knew that the adults around you needed to be more specific to guarantee a desired result; however, you probably had no idea why.

You might think that this is the type of affirmation to use in all scenarios. After all, don't we generally want things to happen right away? That is usually the case, but these types of emergency affirmations don't always work. The previous affirmation categories work every single time, without fail, because they realign your body and mind to be attuned with the object of your desires. With emergency affirmations, there simply isn't enough time for this process to reach completion. The emergency affirmation works more or less along the lines of a prayer. That is, you're asking that—if it's in the interests of your highest good— this thing come to you now. You're letting God, the universe, or whomever know that you're in need of Divine intervention at this particular moment. Obviously, sometimes the answer is going to be no.

Our lives are far too complex for us to see the entire picture. We rely on the Divine to see what we need and then provide it. Sometimes, though, a bit of a push from us can jump-start the process. We, as humans, are blessed with free will. The universe can intervene on our behalf when we ask, and if it's part of the Divine contract we signed before we came to Earth, then it will happen anyway, as a kind of fateful occurrence, if you will. When we use an emergency affirmation, we're signaling that we're open to this help and need it now. This frees the universe to act on our behalf without risk of interfering with our free will—a rule that is never broken.

A combination of these three types of affirmations, with a healthy dose of precise visualization, can lead to untold wealth for you—not just materially, but spiritually as well. Studies have shown that people who use affirmations regularly feel much more connected and at peace with their higher selves. That's because they really take a hand as co-creator of their world and their lives. The seeming randomness of the universe is more clearly understood to be the sacred and intricate dance that it really is.

So try out some affirmations and see how much abundance you can create in your life!

Stay Positive

Positivity is the language of Heaven. When we speak and think in uplifting ways, we're having a direct conversation with our Creator. The Angels of Abundance are delighted when we choose to look at all situations as potentially positive. After all, everything is happening according to a Divine plan, so the end result is, of course, positivity.

We recognize this instinctively. How many times has someone said to you, "We'll laugh about this later"? That's an inherent acknowledgment that all things are destined to work out for the best in the end. God and the angels really are looking out for our highest good at all times, and a bright outlook is nothing more than recognition of this fact.

When we remain positive about our manifestations, we can realize much stronger, and more significant, gains. The optimism and enthusiasm that we possess translates directly into more effective manifestation sessions. Conversely, if we lose that positivity and start doubting the effectiveness of our practice— or start feeling negative about the work that we're trying to do— we can stall progress or even impede it completely.

The reason behind this shift, based on our positivity or negativity, has to do with the energy that our thoughts and words possess. As we've mentioned, positive words have a much higher degree of energy than negative ones. This means that your positive thoughts and emotions lend energy to your manifestation work, and indeed every aspect of your life, and lead to much higher levels of effectiveness.

On the other hand, negative thoughts and emotions carry very little energy. This means that, while negativity is not outright harmful or dangerous, it's quite useless.

On a practical level, positivity can lead to more fulfilling relationships with other people. Very few individuals want to spend much time with those who are negative. Such people can drag down the mood of everyone around them. When we strive to stay positive, not only do we tend to have more energy, but we're also much more pleasant to be around.

Obviously, staying positive just for the sake of keeping people around isn't the primary goal of—and should not be the only reason for—staying positive. Every single area of your life can be improved by a positive mind-set. Your health, your happiness, and even your level of prosperity can be dramatically enhanced by shifting your focus to notice all the joyful events and occurrences that arise, rather than focusing solely on the downside.

It can be difficult to stay positive in the face of adversity, but it's not impossible. Health, happiness, and wealth aside, staying positive is simply more beneficial for your *life*. If you embark on a venture with an optimistic feeling and attitude, you're much more likely to succeed. Whoever heard of anyone starting something new, knowing that it's going to fail, and still giving it 100 percent? When we revert to negativity, we're effectively sabotaging ourselves.

Failing to acknowledge danger or potentially negative situations doesn't do anyone any good. Staying positive doesn't mean living in your own underwater bubble city, oblivious to the world around you. Yes, it's a good idea to avoid doom-and-gloom news shows or articles, but staying completely uninformed about the world isn't an abundance-inspiring habit. If a situation is potentially dangerous or hostile, ignoring that fact won't improve matters. You must be realistic in order to stay happy, healthy, and wealthy. Being realistic, however, doesn't have to transform into negativity.

How can we stay positive when we may be surrounded by a negative world? Easy:

- The **first** step is *not to think* of the world as negative. There are certainly numerous problems, but they're not insurmountable. Most of the world's challenges are human-made and can be human-solved. By acknowledging that we can fix any problem, given enough thoughtful care, we find it much easier to avoid the trap of despair.

- The **second** step is to keep track of all the beauty, goodness, and blessings that you notice around you. Lord knows, enough of the world's negative actions are chronicled, so why not the positive?

This documenting of goodness is called a "gratitude journal." This may give you visions of a love-in back in the '60s, but it's really a valuable tool to help you stay positive. You don't have to do any more with it than you want to. A gratitude journal can be as old-fashioned as a leather-bound tome where you fastidiously keep notes, or as streamlined as an application on your smartphone. Yes, there's an app for that! At first, you may not notice or remember every single bit of goodness that comes your way, but that's perfectly fine. The more you use a gratitude journal, the more you *will* notice.

At a certain point, you may question whether all this goodness has always been there—or is more coming to you because you are, at last, acknowledging its presence? Like much of life, the answer is "all of the above." Yes, there have always been wonderful and beautiful things in this world, but they have a tendency to be overshadowed by the negative and dangerous ones. But just as like attracts like, the more you align yourself with good, the more good will come to you.

If this all sounds *too* good to be true, you should ask yourself why you believe that to be the case. Yes, we do live in a cynical world, and some people will try to take advantage of your trusting nature, but that is not the way of God and the universe. Our Divine Creator wants us to be abundant and happy, just as we want the same for *our* children. The only thing limiting us is the belief that we're in this world by ourselves.

Stay Motivated!

Losing motivation can be a serious impediment to your manifestation work. You can lose motivation when you feel that you're not making progress quickly enough. If your friends and family aren't being supportive, that can also make it easier to let your ambitions wane. Staying positive will help you retain that inner drive. If you have doubts about your progress, consult your gratitude journal. You'll quickly notice that the number of positive things in your life has drastically increased.

If you feel that your friends and family aren't being supportive enough, then speak with them. Most likely, they're not even aware that you feel this way and will take steps to resolve the situation. You don't want to simply hope that the situation improves by itself. This is a breakdown in communication, and serves no one. If you keep the communication channels open with your loved ones, you can stop these issues before they become real rifts in your relationships.

Sharing your personal ambitions with those closest to you can be a very uplifting experience. You should never feel guilty or ashamed about what you want to manifest. You, out of everyone you know, are in the best place to know what you need in your life. Other people may have valuable suggestions, but ultimately, only *you* can decide that something is for your highest good.

If you feel that you've lost the motivation to continue your manifestation work, one great tool to use is a "vision board." As we touched upon in the previous chapter, this is a poster you make consisting of pictures and positive words representing your short- or long-term goals. You can post images of a beautiful home, symbols of wealth such as fancy cars or jewelry, and positive affirmations about your abundance.

Whenever you look at your vision board, you will be reminded of what you want to achieve and, hopefully, will see that your continued perseverance is worth the effort. If you don't see something that really motivates you on the board, then tear down the uninspiring pictures and put up others that will really get you fired up.

The act of being positive has a cumulative effect on your life. The more positive, motivated, and enthusiastic you are in general, and in your manifestations specifically, the more success and happiness you'll be able to achieve. While it's certainly possible for negative people to achieve success, it would have been easier for them if they'd maintained a positive attitude.

In real-world applications, a person's attitude can open and close many doors. When trying to find a new job, eyeing a promotion, or transferring among departments at a traditional employer, a great deal of weight is placed on a person's overall attitude toward work and life in general. Even when people are self-employed, they have much more success dealing with customers and suppliers when they stay positive.

We're not saying that you can never have a bad day or have to pretend to be positive all the time. This is most certainly not the case. We understand all too well that life can sometimes interfere with our intentions. When anyone is confronted with bad news or a sudden twist of fate, it can be easy to slip into a negative state of mind. Just be aware of those times, and try to limit their scope.

When you're conscious of your state of mind, you can establish a realistic view of your life. In that case, you can see for yourself where your energy is being expended. For example, if you're fully aware of when you're being positive and when you're being negative, then you can determine the effect that each of these attitudes has on your life. At that point, you're more qualified to make an informed choice about how you will react to any situation.

Yes, you can choose how you react. It may seem that you merely react to situations in the most appropriate manner at the time, but that moment is your choice, just as any others are. Think back on a particularly stressful situation you were involved in, and try imagining how someone you really respect would have responded. Would this person have reacted in a more positive or more negative way, or in a manner similar to yours?

The point of that reflection is to see that there's no "most appropriate" reaction to any given event. The only gauge of appropriateness is how you feel. If you feel guilty or sick over your reaction, then it wasn't the right choice for you. On the other hand, if you feel uplifted and good, then you made the correct decision.

You can train yourself to react in ways that you consciously choose. You can do this by taking very small steps toward being constantly aware that you are, in fact, making a choice. So the next time you're faced with a stressful or surprising situation, try this: Breathe before acting. Take five to ten seconds to calm and center yourself before you have any outward reaction. Once you've done so, see if you still feel inclined to behave in the same manner you would have initially.

If that seems overly simplistic to you, ask yourself why you believe that to be so. You train yourself by repeatedly performing tasks. In this case, you're just trying to train yourself to think before acting. Nothing could be simpler. Once you're skilled in this art, then you're free to make any decisions with full awareness.

Most people find that, when they start becoming aware—not only of the consequences of a choice, but of the fact that they have a choice at all—they will choose correctly more often. Not coincidentally, the correct choice almost universally is to react to each situation in a more positive manner. Not only is it usually much more successful, but it also *feels* better. The idea of getting really angry at people and letting them "have it" may be temporarily fun or satisfying in some way, but the truth is that it rarely feels good in the long term if we're honest with ourselves.

The bridge between positive thoughts and positive actions is easy to cross. For most people, what they primarily choose with one usually translates to the other. For example, it's almost unheard of for someone who consistently thinks positively to regularly act negatively. That thought-action mismatch can last for a time, but it will eventually be overridden. Our thoughts become our actions, and just as often, our actions can become our thoughts.

Everyone has a set of default actions that they typically engage in. These patterns come about through a combination of past experiences, upbringing, moral values, and overall personality predilections. Actions that are in line with one's personality generally are performed much faster and with less effort. They're more akin to habits than conscious choices. Conversely, behavior that goes against one's personality can cause a thought-action mismatch.

Going through a thought-action mismatch isn't necessarily a bad thing. In some circumstances, we've allowed ourselves to be preprogrammed with a set of actions that do not serve either us or the world. When we recognize that this is the case, we must realign ourselves to a new set of default actions.

The desire to align ourselves more positively is a common one. For example, some people gradually come to the conclusion that they're angrier than they'd like to be. Realizing that becoming calmer and happier would not only improve their interpersonal relationships, but also improve their health, longevity, and level of abundance, they make an effort to change their personalities. And it's not just harmful personality traits, such as anger, that people wish to change. If you've ever felt that you're too passive or accommodating, or possess any other characteristic that's no longer serving you, you can change that.

Realigning personality traits is a surprisingly easy task. With a small amount of discipline, even the most ingrained impulses can be modified. Countless stories have been published about very negative people who had epiphanies and turned their lives completely around. These people weren't special in a way that the rest of us are not. They simply wanted to change profoundly and attract more positive individuals and circumstances into their lives.

The first step to any type of transformation is awareness. If you recognize something about yourself that you'd like to change, you've already completed the most important and, in some ways, the most difficult step toward attaining that goal. The next step is to gradually become more conscious of those times when you display a behavior that no longer serves you.

When you recognize the attitude underlying your actions, you can choose to interrupt your thought-action flow and introduce a new element into it. Rather than act in a negative manner that would otherwise have been your default, you can instead experiment with a more positive option. The result of this little experiment will probably remind you to stay positive, even when things start to feel as if they're sliding in the other direction.

The most important thing to remember is that you're not alone. Your Divine Creator, the angels, your friends, and your family are all supporting you every step of the way. There's no situation that cannot be improved by a positive outlook. Your positivity and forward-thinking attitude through the words and choices you affirm are investments that you're making in yourself.

MESSAGE 9

KEEP YOUR FOCUS

In the preceding chapters, we've spoken about keeping your focus during visualization and affirmations. So you may be thinking, *Haven't they gone over this already?* However, to the Angels of Abundance, this is such an important topic that it warrants a chapter of its very own.

Focus is the key to all manifestation and, hence, the key to all abundance. Even though we advise you to be as specific as possible when you manifest and say your affirmations, focus is what ensures that you'll receive exactly what you want. Keeping your focus can be tricky at times, especially if you're new to manifestation. Numerous books have been written on the topic of increasing attention span and the various disorders that seem to prevent any sort of long-term focus. However, anyone—regardless of physical or emotional state—can focus long enough to perform simple visualizations and affirmations. The key is to use certain tools and techniques to help you along the way.

Focusing Tools and Techniques

For most people, the first essential tool is a simple pen and pad of paper. Keeping extensive notes will not only help you remember what you want to focus on, but can also be an important tool to help you track your progress. Every affirmation you want to perform, everything you want to visualize, should go onto that pad of paper. How you organize this material is completely up to you.

We cannot emphasize enough how much keeping notes will help you in the days and weeks ahead. It can be incredibly easy to put off this simple chore, but detailing what worked for you and what did not will help you hone your focus to a razor's edge. The very act of keeping notes, by itself, will go a long way toward improving your focus.

When you sit down to write down your thoughts and activities, you're exercising not only your memories, but also the parts of your brain that allow you to focus on one single task. If you naturally have a hard time focusing, this simple exercise may take a bit longer. That's perfectly fine; no one's going to keep track of your speed.

If you like to say multiple affirmations a week on a rotating basis, writing them down, along with the corresponding days that you want to use them, is a good idea. This will help you focus on the affirmation itself, rather than figuring out which one you're saying each day. For your visualization, if you cut out or draw a picture of what you'd like—or a close representation, in cases of job advancement and less tangible goods—it will help you get right into the visualization, rather than trying to remember exactly what the object of your desire looks like.

Candles

Other simple objects can help you retain your focus as well. In the *Angel Blessings Candle Kit,* we illustrated how using a candle can help you keep your mind focused on your goals. Candles have been lit in temples and churches for centuries because they are representative of the light of faith. Candles also function as wonderful focal points so that you can focus your mind and emotions on your desires without the ego distracting you with fears.

The advantage of a candle is that it's a physical object that you can hold in your hand. You know it's there because you can see it and feel it. This lends credibility to your affirmations, in your subconscious. Also, you can use specific candles for each object or goal you've chosen to manifest, so your complete focus is on that one goal, which helps prevent your mind from drifting.

The basic method for using a candle as a focusing device is laid out in these easy-to-remember steps:

1. Choose a small candle that has never been used before. If you know the color you'd like to use for your specific purposes, use that. Otherwise, choose a white candle.

2. Clean the candle in a small bowl of saltwater (you can make your own, or use seawater, if available). Dry thoroughly.

3. Hold the candle, and imagine the goal that you'd like to achieve. If it's a specific item, try to picture it completely contained inside the candle, waiting to burst out.

4. Light the candle and allow it to burn down completely. Feel free to recite an affirmation at this point, or simply meditate on the object of your desires. This works especially well at bath times.

That's all it takes to use candles for manifestation. There are a few advanced techniques involving dressing the candle in oil, watching the way the flames flicker, and using specific colors and types of wax, but that is beyond the scope of this book.

Crystals

Crystals are another device you can use to help you keep focused. Like candles, they're physical items that you can hold, so you're more able to focus on the practical applications of what you're doing. Some crystals serve a dual purpose, because they can also amplify and focus the manifestation work that you're already doing.

The safest, easiest, and most affordable crystal to obtain for manifestation purposes is the clear quartz crystal. Don't worry about the size, shape, or clarity for this exercise. If you're lucky enough to live in an area where quartz is naturally abundant, you can simply pick up one of the rocks that you find lying about. If you have a particularly cherished stone, feel free to use that as well. The following steps are simple but can prove very effective, even for people who've never used crystals for manifestation before:

1. Clean your crystal, either by dipping it into saltwater (a solution mixed by hand or seawater) or by setting your crystal out in the light of the full moon.

2. Visualize the object of your desire in as much detail as you can manage.

3. Imagine that the object you're visualizing is passing through the crystal; and the crystal is acting as a

lens to make the picture larger, brighter, and in sharper focus.

4. Repeat an affirmation, while holding the crystal, as many times as you wish.

Obviously, there are many more potential steps you can take with crystals. As we stated earlier, they're a body of work unto themselves. You can make working with them as complicated or as simple as you please. In this book, we're choosing simplicity, because the more rules you apply to yourself or allow others to apply to you, the higher the likelihood that you'll forget them. It's much more important for the manifestation beginner to focus on what really matters—in this case, visualizations, affirmations, and goals, rather than arcane principles. You won't anger any beings or manifest in a "wrong" way if you keep it simple and stick to the four steps outlined above. If you're guided to add or remove any steps, please feel free to do so. The best method is the one that works for you.

Yoga, Tai Chi, and Meditation

Beyond physical items, such as candles and pads of paper, there are exercises you can perform that will help you focus on your life and manifestations. Yoga is an increasingly popular method for sculpting the body and sharpening the mind, and we do recommend this practice if you feel that it's right for you. Other people benefit more from regular tai chi sessions. This activity has the added benefit of being freely available in public parks worldwide. If there's a public park of sufficient size in your town or city, there's a very good chance that tai chi groups meet on a regular basis during warm-weather months. The reason yoga and tai chi can help you improve your focus is that, in addition to being wonderful exercises for the body, they're also meditative in nature. Meditating in any form helps bring the mind into sharp focus through training. While it's perfectly acceptable and quite beneficial to simply meditate, doing so in a yoga or tai chi setting has the added value of physical exercise, which promotes increased concentration and memory retention when performed regularly. The benefits will be cumulative when exercise and meditation are paired together. (You'll find some guided meditations in the Appendix.)

Renewing Your Focus

There will be times when you lose your focus, regardless of how well trained your mind is, how thorough your notes are, and how centered you may be. Don't panic when this happens; it's perfectly natural. Your subconscious is simply telling you that you should focus on something else at this time. Sometimes you're meant to think about the distracting thoughts that enter your mind. Take a moment to sort through them, and if any need to be taken care of right away, go ahead and do so. The rest will quiet down with contemplation and acknowledgment, and you'll be able to go back to your manifestation work with a clear head and a focused mind. Losing focus is not the end of the world; it's simply an opportunity to reevaluate your priorities at that particular moment.

The difference between a manifestation technique performed with a focused mind and one done with an unfocused mind is similar to the difference between music played by a master and that played by a first-year student. The manifestation is still being carried out regardless, but with far more efficiency and better results when there's focus. This is why we encourage you to figure out what's diverting your attention and eliminate it from your mind as soon as possible.

If you just try to power through the visualization or affirmation while thinking about how the laundry needs to be done, the kids need to be fed, and the dog needs to be walked, you'll essentially be wasting your time. You owe it to yourself to be fully focused whenever you set out to manifest the abundance that's coming your way.

When you find your mind cluttered with a to-do list of other tasks that can be safely left until later, a simple way to focus is to say this quick blessing to yourself: "My life is one of abundance—an abundance of joy, love, and blessings—and free of any worry. I grow this abundance to help make the world a better place."

This simple blessing reminds you that it's okay to be abundant, that you're *already* abundant, and that you want nothing but goodness for everyone. Tasks that can wait are put aside, because you're focused on a much bigger project at that moment. You're a very important person and must allow yourself the time it takes to do the job properly.

Starting today, and continuing for as long as it takes to feel comfortable, repeat this blessing. You may wish to make a little note, check mark, or number in your journal every day that you repeat it. Think of how you feel the very first time you say it. Compare that to how you feel the tenth day you say it. See how long it takes you to actually believe it. At that point, you'll really be able to maintain your focus, no matter what others tell you or what you've previously told yourself.

This chapter is called "Keep Your Focus," but it could have been called "Give Yourself Permission," because that's really what keeping your focus is. It's your mind giving you permission to be as abundant as you want to be. There will always be an excuse or something better that you could be doing, but by giving yourself permission, you're reminding yourself that it's just as important to look after *you* as everyone else around you. Instead of thinking about all the things that you could be doing instead—or about how guilty you feel for taking time for yourself—think about all the good things you'll be able to do with the abundance that you're working so hard to obtain. Ultimately, you and everyone else around you will be much better off, because you took time out of your busy schedule for self-care.

As part of your habit of keeping notes, it's a good practice to take a moment, now and again, to brainstorm new ideas. Every single device or service that you use during the day started out as a single idea in someone's head. That person is no different from you. He or she just pushed ahead with that idea, despite others saying how it could fail. Once you come up with great ideas, you can start focusing on them, visualizing them, and affirming that the ideas are realities that are making people happy and making you lots of well-deserved income.

Creative Manifestation

Nearly every single part of the day can be used to manifest abundance in some manner or another. You're constantly surrounded by the wonder of creation, and *you* can also create. When you've trained your mind to the point that you can focus on what you want, regardless of external distractions, you'll be able to easily take five minutes to do a quick visualization, wherever you happen to be. Suppose you're stuck in a dull meeting that has absolutely nothing whatsoever to do with your job responsibilities (don't laugh, it *does* happen). Well, that's a perfect time to silently repeat affirmations or to visualize the object of your desire. Not only will this ground and center you, but it will also make the time you're spending in this meeting worthwhile.

When you practice manifesting during times when you would otherwise be idle, you reclaim so-called wasted time. If you keep track of how much time you're able to snatch away for manifestation, you might be quite surprised by how many moments you've managed to get back.

As we stated earlier, a lot of this work is residual, so you may not notice the effects right away, and you may not immediately notice the effects diminishing when you stop practicing. One of the most important aspects of manifestation, therefore, must be consistency of focus.

We won't go so far as to say that stopping right when things start working for you would be *foolish*, but it would waste some of your efforts. Once you start back up again, you'll have to wait out the lag time until things start working again. It would be far better to simply continue your practice without interruption than to constantly stall and restart. This will not only save time, but also keep your mind accustomed to using all the manifestation tools at your disposal. Continually maintaining your practice is the most effective way to keep your focus.

ALLOW YOURSELF
TO RECEIVE

You could read a thousand prosperity books and attend a hundred workshops about the Law of Attraction. But until you allow yourself to receive, none of those principles will help you to manifest your supply.

As you follow the messages from the Angels of Abundance, magic will start to occur in your life. You will be offered opportunities, come up with new brilliant ideas, and feel inspired to go for your dreams. This is where you must overcome the ego's fears about receiving. Otherwise, your ego will sabotage all of your good efforts and block you once again from manifesting the abundance you desire and deserve.

You will begin to notice gifts in many different forms. These gifts could include people offering to help you, finding money in a series of places, and new ideas coming to you. When these gifts arrive, the magical phrase for you to use is: "Thank you." That's right, simply offer thanks and graciously accept the good coming to you.

Of course, if your gut feelings sound alarms that you can't trust the person who's offering you something, you will want to meditate and pray: *"Dear God, I'm not certain whether it's the ego or my higher self warning me. Please protect me from any negative influences."* But in most cases, doing all the great work you've been doing will only bring people of the highest integrity and welcome opportunities to you.

It's Safe for You to Receive

You (like everyone) deserve happiness, health, abundance, love, and success. The lower self (ego) is based on fear, so it's threatened by happiness. The ego tries to persuade you that you don't deserve to receive, and that success will bring about increased responsibilities, pressures, and changes in your relationships. Your higher self happily accepts support, knowing that this is sustenance for its life purpose.

When you receive, you're more able to help others. For instance, if you let yourself be paid for your healing, teaching, artistic, or spiritually based work, then you can leave a less meaningful job. This will allow you to devote more time and resources to helping others.

You're not taking away from anyone else when you allow yourself to receive. You're actually building a supply of energy, self-esteem, and strength that you'll pass along to others. Your talents, passions, and interests are the foundation of your life purpose.

Here are some angel affirmations to support your healthy changes:

- *It is safe for me to receive.*

- *I now live my life according to my inner guidance.*

- *It is safe for me to be happy.*

- *I enjoy and deserve peace.*

- *I have compassion for myself.*

- *I trust and listen to my feelings.*

- *I am loved and supported.*

- *It is safe for me to be successful.*

- *I allow myself to receive love and support.*

- *It is safe to be my authentic self with other people.*

- *I have the right to change my life to mirror my higher self's visions.*

- *I easily let go of the old when its purpose has been served.*

- *I take excellent care of myself in all ways.*

- *When I win, everybody wins.*

Saying these affirmations daily (either out loud or silently) will boost your self-esteem, confidence, energy, and motivation.

Seagulls and Driftwood

When your dream is coming true, it's a lot like a sailor seeing signs of land nearby. At first you will receive little gifts from the universe that are in the direction of your dream. This is just like the sailor spying a seagull or driftwood to know that he is near land. What if the sailor said that the seagull and the driftwood weren't good enough, and he threw a fit because his dream of coming to shore wasn't true right now? What if he completely lost faith in his dream of reaching land, gave up all hope, and stopped sailing right there and then?

This metaphor illustrates the all-too-common practice of giving up five minutes before the miracle. It's essential to keep your mind clear, and aware of the small signs that your dream is coming to you. The little gifts from the universe are your seagulls and driftwood. Keep sailing in the direction of those gifts, and you will find your dream there!

Balancing Giving and Receiving

In this physical 3-D world of duality and polarities, opposites exist and balance themselves. One of the opposites that is evident throughout nature is giving and receiving. Examples include the tide of the ocean going in and out, and inhaling and exhaling breath. Many sensitive and gentle people are more comfortable giving than receiving. But both are equally important. If you only give, you will block yourself from receiving abundance. Being receptive also opens you up to better hearing—and accept—Divine guidance. If you only give, you are blocking all forms of receptivity.

Giving is a male energy, and receiving is a female energy. It's essential that we all balance giving and receiving every day in order to balance the male and female energies within us.

Masculine energy is about power, authority, control, and getting yourself out there in the world. Feminine energy is about nurturing, intuition, and feelings. Everyone, whether a man or woman, has both male and female energies present. Feminine energy is the artist, and masculine energy is the artist's manager and agent.

In any relationship, it's important that both partners are givers and receivers. Have you ever been in a relationship with someone who would only *take* from you? Or have you known someone who refused to accept help? Imbalanced people are frustrating to be around, so you don't want to do that to others by being just a giver or a taker.

Every day, do your best to balance giving and receiving. Allow yourself to receive and say thank you for the gifts that come your way. Allow others to help you. Accept compliments and advice.

In balance, be sure that you are also giving to others in equal measure. In fact, you can increase the amount of giving that comes your way by giving more yourself. As long as you're allowing yourself to receive, you can't outgive the universe. everything that you give will always return to you tenfold—that is, as long as you *allow* yourself to receive that tenfold return. Of course, the Angels of Abundance say that we don't give in order to receive. That wouldn't be true giving, after all. Give for the joy of it, and for the fulfillment of being of sacred service whenever and however you can.

Know that you can do a lot of good for others right now. You don't need to wait until you're published, have a healing center, or gain more confidence in order to help others. You have the Divine gift of helping and healing right this very minute. So give, give, give . . . and receive, receive, receive.

KEEP YOUR DIVINE CONTRACT

At the start of this book, we mentioned that this is a work about Divine contracts, which are made between you and your Creator. The angels play a very important role in this Divine contract.

The interesting thing about this agreement is that it's so incredibly one-sided. You're contracting to receive exactly what you ask to receive. You're not expected to reciprocate—except, perhaps, by offering a touch of appreciation and acknowledgment of where your blessings are coming from.

The Angels of Abundance relay your wishes, amendments, and desires to the Universal Power, where they are fulfilled. Throughout this book, you've learned the importance of making sure that the message being passed on is exactly what you'd like it to be. By illustrating the importance of specificity, we aren't trying to scare you; we're merely passing on a truth that you need to be aware of in order to fully understand your choices.

Awareness is the key to so many areas of your life. Without it, you may as well be a drone. All of your choices must be made with the full knowledge of why you're making them. Even if the rationale behind your choices isn't the best, just having a reason and being aware of it are what matter.

One of the trickiest aspects of this subject is how our choices affect other people. It's true that sometimes what we decide can lead to negative consequences for those we care about. The angels teach us, however, that if we're truly aware of the nature of our choices, that will never happen. It is part of our lesson here on Earth to learn how to anticipate the repercussions of our choices and actions, until completion.

Consequences don't ripple outward in a limitless chain of events. Like a stone thrown in a large lake, the energy of your actions does eventually return to neutral. This is great news, as the human mind can have trouble with the concept of infinity. This also means that, given enough thoughtful intention, you can reasonably foresee how your choices will impact others.

It is our belief that people who deliberately set out to harm others are very rare. For the most part, people are good-hearted and kind. The majority of hurt and pain caused by our fellow humans is, therefore, unintentional. When we raise our awareness, we act as beacons to show others how to raise their awareness as well.

The Angels of Abundance love it when we model for others how to become more aware of their choices. They always pass on any message we give them, whether we know we're giving it to them or not. When we're more aware, the angels are able to deliver loving messages that will help us immensely. Given the choice, everyone prefers to pass on positive news and requests rather than negative ones.

The Terms of the Contract

The nature of the contracts we make with our Creator can change over time. If we come to an epiphany and decide that the current track of our lives is unacceptable to us—or needs to be improved in some way—we are free to change that. Using the tools outlined in this book, it's possible to effortlessly attract abundance in every area of life.

The nature of time, as it exists on our planet, is a purely human construct. Because you've lived your life in a set pattern for so long, you may believe that it will take you a proportionate amount of time to *change* your life. That is simply not true. Your life is assisted by Divine beings who are not limited by space and time in any way. They can help you move your life in a positive and fulfilling direction *now*. However, like all contracts, you must give something back in return.

What could you, as a human with a physical body, possibly give to a spiritual being who is without limits? After all, these beings could have anything they desire, at any time, *if* they even desired anything at all. The nature of value only exists for humans, because of the finite nature of our physical plane. The spiritual plane has no such limitations, so the idea of giving something back may sound ludicrous. There is, fortunately for us, one very important thing we can offer in return for Divine assistance, and that valuable offering is called *permission*. God, the angels, and all of the Divine beings cannot act on your behalf unless you ask for help. Your right to self-rule and free will is without limit, for all eternity. Even if these otherwise limitless creations desired to subvert your free will (and they, of course, *never* wish to do that), they would be incapable of doing so.

We were put on this planet for a very important reason. And although each person's purpose is different, it invariably involves being able to make choices. We're faced with a thousand reasons to ignore our Divine purpose every single day, so what makes us great contributors to the world is our ability to ignore those temptations. We can turn off the television, put down the game controller, and say no to that night out at the club.

You do not, of course, need to shut yourself off from life. A monastic existence may be fulfilling for some, but it's not what the majority of us were put here on Earth to accomplish. However, you do need to be able to focus on your own projects and keep out potential negativity while you re-create your life in abundant new ways.

You will know instantly whether or not you're in a positive contract because when you find yourself in one, you will do your very best to ignore anyone around you who tells you that all good things must come to an end. The Sufi mantra of "This too shall pass" may be true, but when we're speaking of

Divine contracts, when one ends, another immediately begins. The good times of positivity, abundance, and love need never have to come to an end.

The goal of all of these Divine contracts is to help you fine-tune your life so that external distractions don't keep you from focusing on your purpose. The angels do not want mundane details, such as worry and lack, to interfere with the lessons you're here to learn. They will absolutely help you with any area of your life where you feel you can use their assistance. You simply have to swallow your pride and ask for help.

From time to time, it seems that we're asking for help over and over again, and that our need is so great that we can't understand why none is forthcoming. This is simply a misunderstanding, due to a difference in perspective on the situation. We are, of necessity, active participants in our lives. We see things from a first-person perspective, and it can be very difficult to step into the third-person point of view. God and the angels aren't limited in this regard. They can see every single aspect of our lives with much greater clarity and wisdom than we can imagine.

If you're genuinely asking for, and are open to, help, then you're getting it. You may not be able to fully see or appreciate the level of help you're receiving at the time, but everything is being put into place for your greatest good.

This can be a tough message to accept at times. It can be easy to confuse what we believe to be best for us and what is *truly* best. This is where faith comes in. We must be able to trust that God and the angels are looking out for us every step of the way.

Don't fret if this is difficult for you. After all, if faith were easy, then it would have no value. It is, by definition, something that you should come by after much contemplation.

Ending or Amending a Contract

Once you're through with a Divine contract, you may end it at any time. If your priorities have realigned for any reason, you may simply switch to a different manifestation. You don't need to wait for each Divine contract to expire successfully before moving on to another one. You can do this in several ways.

— The **first** way to remove an old contract is to simply ask your angels. Any angel will do, although it is a particular specialty of Archangel Michael to cut the cords to your old contract. A cord is essentially a spiritual tie to another object, desire, being, or thought. You develop cords whenever you encounter any of these objects, people, or thoughts. Cords are a method of passing energy between you and everything else in the universe. When they build up too densely, to the point where they're literally draining your energy or you simply no longer need the object in your life, you can ask that they be cut. The severing of these cords can often uplift you, if you have excessive numbers of them, but they never remove any positive influences from your life. And you don't need to be afraid that removing cords to your partner will negatively impact your relationship.

When you cut your cords to an old contract, you're saying to the universe that you no longer wish to expend energy on that task, and you would, instead, like that energy to be redirected to the next contract. There is absolutely no penalty for canceling a Divine contract early.

— The **second** method for canceling an old contract that no longer serves you is a bit more esoteric. It's perfect for those among us who work better with physical objects and symbols than with intangible thoughts. With this method, you write down exactly what you were trying to manifest or attract into your life. You may be as detailed or as general as you wish.

This process is for your own comfort and peace of mind, rather than being a secret ritual that must be done in the proper order and way.

Once you've written down what you were previously trying to attract, you then bury that piece of paper under earth of any sort. Any regular wood-based sheet of paper will biodegrade in a matter of days, which will completely remove any residual remnant of that old contract from your life forever.

You may restart a Divine contract if, for any reason, you change your mind. Even one that has been canceled for some time may be reopened and the manifestation process continued. If you remember precisely what you were previously trying to attract, you may simply ask the angels to help you reach your goal. Otherwise, you can repeat your earlier manifestation following whatever technique you used before. This should be much easier this time, as you've already been through the process.

The word *contract* can sound scary to some people. In this instance, you have nothing to fear. You won't owe anyone anything throughout this Divine contract. At no point will you be subject to any penalties for lack of action on your part. You're free to enter and leave this Divine contract as you choose. This is a Divine contract of unconditional love that will help you achieve all of your heart's desires.

The Angels of Abundance absolutely want you to ask them for help, and they want you to know that. They have infinite patience and will wait for your request. You never have to worry that you're bothering them, and there are no limitations on how many places they can be at once. If you ask for their assistance, it doesn't mean they would be unable to aid someone else with a more dire need. They can help, and are helping, everyone with equal tenacity.

AFTERWORD

Congratulations! You now have a very firm grasp on manifestation in all of its diverse forms. Every area of your life can benefit from the tools and techniques you've just learned. By reading this book in its entirety, you've shown a commitment to not only making your life better in all ways, but to improving the world as a whole.

You came to this planet to fulfill a very powerful mission. God and the angels, especially the Angels of Abundance that you've been working with so closely, are helping you every step of the way. Now that you know how to invite them in and ask them for the help you need, your mission is that much closer to being fulfilled.

The Angels of Abundance are fulfilling *their* mission by helping you to fulfill *your* mission. They are happy that you've taken the time to understand the ways in which they're here to help you. They don't want you to experience any physical suffering due to lack. They want you to be able to complete your mission and help as many people as possible.

The most effective manifestation tool in the universe is *the one that works for you.* We strongly encourage you to try all of the techniques you've learned at least once, and see what you're most comfortable with. If you enjoy them all, that's fantastic. If, on the other hand, you feel strongly drawn to one, then by all means favor that one to the exclusion of the others. You're under no obligation to use any technique that you find unworkable or uncomfortable.

In the Introduction, we stated that this is a book about Divine contracts. That remains true to the end. Your side of the Divine contract now requires that you practice in order to get results. You're equipped with the knowledge and the motivation to manifest whatever you desire. It's now up to you to go forward and make that happen. The Angels of Abundance are only able to help you when you ask them to. Calling upon them regularly is the ideal method of ensuring that you're never without their loving help and guidance.

Remaining open to the gifts that God and the Angels of Abundance are bringing you is a critical piece of manifestation. You must learn to instinctively trust that the abundance coming your way is a gift from the Divine. When opportunity knocks, don't pause to consider whether you deserve it or are worthy of it. *You absolutely are.* Sometimes, as in the case of job interviews or amazing deals on something you were going to purchase anyway, there's a distinct time limit involved. You must be ready to strike while the iron is hot, as the old saying goes.

If you do accidentally let one of these opportunities slip by, don't despair or panic. There will be more where they came from. Once you start on the road to manifestation, it can almost feel as if there's a conspiracy to make you successful and abundant. Obviously, the more closely attuned you are to noticing these opportunities as they come up, the better off you'll be, but you should never berate yourself for missing something.

We encourage you to designate a journal for your personal use. In this journal, you can write about your manifestation efforts and experiences. You can, for instance, chronicle each abundant manifestation that comes to you as you use these techniques.

Journaling helps with manifestation because it serves as a reminder. For example, if you were to chronicle 40 days of mani- festing and 40 days of success, you would instantly know why nothing happened on that 41st day, when you forgot to use your affirmations or pray.

Meditation is also a very important tool for manifesting abundance. (We've included some guided meditations in the Appendix, along with some true manifestation stories to inspire you on your journey.)

Last, it would not be a joint Virtue book if we didn't include a little blurb about balance, which is the key to a fulfilled life. Throughout your journey, you must strive to ensure that you're not giving disproportionate amounts of time or energy to any one area. Abundance and success are very important, it's true, but they're not the most important things in life.

Make doubly sure that you don't spend all of your time working. Go for a walk on a sunny day. Watch a bit of television with someone you care about. Even go so far as to "waste" a little time now and again. We've all seen those people who care for nothing other than work and seek a method of monetizing even the smallest of hobbies. It's not pretty, because it signifies a life that's out of balance.

A balanced life will be of direct benefit to your manifestations. It's not true that someone must work single-mindedly toward a goal in order to achieve success. When your life is balanced in all ways, it allows you to keep the positive mind-set necessary to properly manifest abundance in every way. People who work nonstop may be financially abundant, but at what cost to the abundance in their health and love lives?

We are by no means advocating laziness. Anyone who wants to have any success in manifesting will have to work, and work very hard at times, to reach their financial goals. It's not sufficient to wish for abundance without putting any effort behind it. However, the last thing we want is for the quest for abundance to take over every aspect of your life.

We will leave you with this: We are all made up of equal parts mind, body, and spirit. So, every day, strive to give equal attention to each area of your life . . . and you will achieve perfect balance.

Thank you for reading.

— Doreen and Grant

MANIFESTATION STORIES

We regularly receive letters from people who have had great success with the techniques outlined in this book. In many cases, they only resorted to trying a certain technique due to a perceived emergency or a special circumstance. In an act of desperation, they decided to take a risk and see whether these tools could actually help them.

The results, as you may well imagine, were well worth the effort. When we let go of our ego and decide that we've had enough and that it's okay to ask for help, there is absolutely no limit to how much we can achieve. The only "limited" person in the world—and we mean this in every sense, taking into account all supposed handicaps—is the one who does not ask for help when it's needed.

A man named Thomas wrote to us not too long ago. He explained that he was temporarily out of work because his company had been bought out by a larger competitor that had decided not to keep on any of the staff. As a result, several people in his area were all looking for the same type of job.

Thomas knew, without a doubt, that he was going to find a new position, but in the meantime, he had bills to pay, and he worried that his family would suffer during his career transition. Simple math showed that he didn't have enough in his checking account to satisfy all his outstanding debts, and this was not a very comforting feeling for him.

That very day, Thomas started using affirmations. He repeated to himself, "I am Divinely cared for in all ways. I always have enough to pay my bills."

Thomas apparently believed, as we do, that a simple affirmation can be very effective. He wrote checks to his mortgage lender, credit-card companies, and other firms where he was behind on his payments. He repeated his affirmation as he wrote out each check, and again when he went to mail them.

Two weeks later, the checks hadn't cleared Thomas's account. He wasn't receiving any harassing phone calls yet, so he wasn't quite sure what to make of the situation. As Thomas explained in his letter, he decided that the best thing to do was to call these companies himself, before they decided that his payments hadn't been sent out on time. Each company reported back that they'd received the payments and had posted them to his account. He was completely current, and nothing further needed to be done at that point.

He continued to monitor his bank account, but he couldn't see any evidence that any of the checks had cleared, yet all of the companies assured Thomas that they'd deposited them, crediting his account. However, his bank account didn't reflect this. In the end, what he had affirmed had come true: somehow, he had enough money to pay his bills.

Thomas's story, as remarkable as it sounds, is hardly unique among those who regularly practice some form of manifestation. Regardless of what area of your life you're trying to improve, you'll find that you accomplish what you set out to do virtually every time you use these tools. The reason they work is because they're Divine gifts. They're not subject to human and physical limitations. Time and distance mean nothing to the angels; they're always ready and willing to help you. And you're certainly not limited to the tools we've discussed here. They're simply the ones people find most accessible and helpful. The angels are happy to hear any loving message and call for help, regardless of how the request is made.

A couple of years ago, we received a letter from a woman named Margaret. She told us how she wished to return to college after a two-year break. She wrote that she'd intended to work and raise enough money to finish college during those two years. However, her finances never really caught up to her expenses, and she simply wasn't able to save enough money.

Margaret decided that in order to meet her goal, she had to try something different, so she decided to create a vision board. The board consisted of pictures of new cars, homes with SOLD signs, and various people graduating from college. These images helped Margaret clearly define her goals, as well as keep her mind focused on exactly what she desired so that God and the angels could bring her precisely what she wanted.

Margaret reported that, within three weeks of creating this vision board, she was promoted at work to a management position in a new town. The perks of relocating included a company car, an easy-to-manage home mortgage, and tuition to night school, where she could pursue a management degree.

So you can see that God and the angels aren't limited in any way. Even so, they have a much easier time giving us what we need and desire when we're clear about what we want. When we do so, it becomes that much easier for us to achieve our goals.

The tools for manifesting are very powerful and can be put to use in new and interesting ways. Nothing requires you to use these tools in a prescribed fashion. A letter we received several years ago from a woman named Amanda illustrates this point quite well.

Amanda was home one night, finishing up some work, when the power suddenly went out. Living in a rural area, she was well prepared for such a circumstance. She lit a few emergency candles and was able to ensure that she had everything she needed.

Approximately one hour later, the cause of the power outage made itself known: a very large and noisy lightning storm. Amanda was understandably scared, but she decided she was going to do something about her fear. She took her emergency candles and imagined calm waters, clear skies, and the electricity coming on in her home. Using techniques very similar to those outlined in this book, she turned her ordinary emergency candle into a powerful tool for manifestation.

Shortly after finishing this ritual, the storm moved off. The sky cleared, and Amanda was able to see the stars and the moon. Not long afterward, the power company was able to restore electricity to all the affected homes, and all was well.

Amanda's story shows us how, with very little preparation and the bare minimum of tools, it's possible to manifest our wishes. We don't need to stand on ritual unless it helps us in some way. If the ritual has meaning to you, then it's important; however, if you feel that any part of the process is tedious or meaningless, then it has no use and can be discarded. If all you have is an emergency candle, then what better tool to use in an emergency?

༄ ༄ ༄

We've heard so many times, from so many people, that they're afraid their problem is too trivial for the angels. There has never been a scenario where that was true. Any situation that distracts you from your mission is worthy of help from God and the angels. You never need to worry that you're bothering them. They want to help you and are only waiting for you to ask.

Whenever we find ourselves in a bit of trouble, or are worried about something, the first thing we try to do is ask for help. This hasn't always been easy for us to do. In the past, both of us have been among those people too proud to ask for help, even when we really needed it.

Getting over that hurdle is a common challenge for many. Unfortunately, there really is no easy solution that can magically make you more willing to humble yourself. It's your attitude *toward* help that must be changed. The way in which you arrived at your present belief or preference about asking for assistance is unique, just as you are.

Every single person can get to the place where he or she no longer finds asking for help uncomfortable. Sure, at times you'd rather not because you believe you can do something by yourself just as easily. That isn't the same as being completely shut down to the idea. The only effective method for getting accustomed to this important job is to *keep* asking for help—every single time, if possible. The more you ask, the more comfortable you'll become.

And we can attest to this fact. In both of our cases, it took several years of constantly reminding ourselves to ask before we became comfortable with it.

The reward is, of course, worth the effort. When we ask God and the angels, including the Angels of Abundance, for help, we receive it every single time. As stated previously, the help may not be in an instantly recognizable form, but in the end, you'll receive exactly what you need. If you choose *not* to ask for help, then the level of assistance that God and the angels can give you is drastically limited. All of us were given free will, and that includes the right to try to make it in this world without any Divine intervention whatsoever.

For most people, a life without any help from above is not the type of life they strongly desire for themselves. We cannot state often enough how important and effective simply asking for help is.

A letter we received from a man named Dennis illustrates this point remarkably well. Dennis was a taxi driver and always fancied himself a man's man who could do anything himself.

This assumption was correct most of the time, so he continued to believe it well into old age. However, Dennis reached a stage where doing everything by himself had become increasingly difficult. But despite his need for assistance, he found himself completely incapable of asking for help. Even when it was offered, he still refused, because that would be an admission of weakness, from his point of view.

Fortunately, Dennis was gifted with a wonderful dream, in which his family was all together and happy. In this dream, he was able to help his loved ones, to the best of his ability, and they helped him in return. He was able to see the many ways in which family members were grateful to him for all his years of hard work and dedication, and he, in turn, was reminded of how proud he was of them for being so close to him and willing to help.

From that day forward, Dennis was no longer afraid to ask for help. He would perform those tasks he was able to, but if something was too difficult for him, he would ask for assistance. Eventually, this led him to ask for Divine intervention on behalf of himself and various family members.

Dennis's letter explained that, without that dream, which he credits the angels for giving him, he would probably not have connected so strongly with his family and God. He believes that he might very well have continued on his old path and perhaps not even be alive any longer.

In some ways, Dennis's story is an extreme one, but in other respects, it's something that most of us will face sooner or later. We will all come to a point where we have absolutely no other choice but to ask for help, and we must be comfortable enough to do that without hesitation. Dennis was able to break through that barrier and was rewarded with a fulfilling, comfortable, and safe elderly life. Imagine what sorts of surprises could be in store for you if *you* ask for help.

When requesting help from above, you may, from time to time, be required to act on that which is offered you. If you ask for a new job and are suddenly called for an interview, you can't skip it and then expect to get the job. In a case such as that, you'll have to take the obvious and required steps to meet the universe halfway. In many cases, the help you're given is the equivalent of God opening a door; you merely have to walk through it.

MEDITATIONS
FOR
ABUNDANCE

When you meditate, you can quickly align yourself with the positive energies of abundance. What you focus on during your meditations can directly affect the end result of your manifestations. It is very important, therefore, that you only focus on positive and loving images and thoughts.

This section includes several sample meditations that you can use to start manifesting abundance. Feel free to modify any of these to suit your needs. If there's a specific bit of imagery that you'd like to include, you can either replace parts of the particular meditation or add it to the middle. Before you add anything, however, consider these questions: *Is this imagery as positive as it can be? Am I absolutely certain that I want to manifest this?* If the answer to both of these questions is yes, you can include this imagery without fear.

The first sample meditation calls upon God and the Angels of Abundance, asking them to help you start manifesting your desires. You begin and end this meditation through your breath.

Breathe slowly but deeply, in through the mouth and out through the nose. Repeat this breath seven times. Imagine that, with each breath, you are expelling all fear and doubt from your body, while taking in pure hope and positivity.

Continue breathing slowly, as you call up a picture in your mind of what you would like to manifest. Try to bring this picture to life with as much detail as possible. See every aspect of your desire as if it is physical. Hold this picture in your mind, ignoring all external distractions. The only thing that is real, at this moment, is your picture and your breath.

While still holding this picture in your mind, mentally or verbally say the following:

*"God and the Angels of Abundance, I ask for your
help to continue on my life path without physical distraction
and discomfort. I realize that my path is a powerful one,
and I would like to focus completely upon it without worry.*

*"I trust that God and the angels will help me with these goals,
as they help everyone who asks. I have no doubt or fear in my heart.
Please ensure that my desires and needs are met in all ways.*

*"Thank you, God and Angels of Abundance, for providing
such loving bounty now. I reaffirm my desire to continue the
path that God and I have chosen to better the planet
in the most effective way.
Amen."*

*Now, simply be at peace and focus on your breath. Every
breath is a gift from God and reminds you that you are abundantly provided for in so many different ways. To God, all
abundance is the same. God and the angels will provide
equally for all.*

*Stay at peace, and breathe for as long as you wish. You
may end this meditation at any time, and repeat it as many*

times as you would like. This is not the place for fear or doubt. Know that it is an absolute truth that God and the angels will do what is best for you, now that you have asked for their help.

It's important to note that you can think of more than one object or concept to manifest during your meditations. The only limitation here stems from your own ego. The power of the Divine is limitless, so you shouldn't limit yourself. If you wish for a great new home, car, and job, then by all means try to manifest all three at the same time. You don't need to wait for one manifestation to come into physical being before starting on the next.

If you're having trouble focusing on multiple desires at once, then simply perform this meditation as many times as the number of wishes you have. You simply need to stay positive, have faith, and remember to ask, and all of your physical wants and needs will be taken care of.

If there's something very specific that you'd like, such as a particular home you've had your eye on, then specificity can be very helpful. When you picture the home in your mind, visualize the outside walls. Imagine what it would feel like to actually touch them. Ask yourself: *What does the house feel like? Does it have a backyard?* Picture yourself mowing the lawn, and imagine the feeling you'd have while doing so.

All those added touches make the picture more real and believable to you. And the more real this is, the easier it is to bring it into physical being. This happens because you're more likely to believe that the picture in your mind is real if you can make it *feel* real. Real objects are things you can see, touch, smell, taste, and hear. If this picture in your mind can address all five senses, there's nothing separating it from what is physically real.

You can see, then, that when you meditate, you will nearly always utilize the techniques learned in earlier chapters. This whole-body approach toward manifestation has been proven, several times over, to be the most effective method currently known. Eventually, new methods will be discovered, and results can and do vary, depending on the individual. With enough practice, you'll discover which methods of manifestation you're most comfortable with.

Grant: The following meditation was kindly donated to this project by my wife, Melissa Virtue. Melissa has performed these lovely meditations for audiences around the world. On our weekly radio show, she regularly guides listeners through similar meditations. She has specifically written this meditation for you, the reader of this book. Enjoy!

Find a comfortable, quiet place where you can relax. Either sit or lie down with your palms open to the sky. Close your eyes.

Inhale deeply. Exhale, releasing all air. Repeat this two more times.

In your mind's eye, see a glowing emerald-green light moving up from the earth into the bottoms of your feet. This light feels warm and soothing. As you continue to inhale and exhale, allowing the rhythm of your breath to flow, feel the emerald light move up into your legs, hips, pelvis area, stomach, and rib cage, and settle into your heart space. Feel this warm light cleanse and clear your heart space. It feels as if your heart is expanding with each inhale and exhale.

Now, see a shimmering silver ball of light floating down into the crown of your head, down into your throat area, and settling into your heart space, where it fuses with the green light. You can feel this beautiful silvery-green light pulsating as it opens, aligns, and balances your heart chakra.

As the light continues to connect you to the earth and sky, you see, in your mind's eye, a stone archway before you. Notice the lush growth of flowers and plants along this gateway. Take a moment to see your name etched at the top of the arch. Next to your name you can read "Receives Abundance Now." This is your personal gateway to allowance. Your choice to cross this threshold is a resounding yes to the universe. It tells the Divine Source that you are, in fact, ready to receive your abundance now. You are willing to open up to your bliss in all areas of your life. You are willing to allow the highest good into your life.

Stepping through this archway, you discover a golden pathway.

Standing on this pathway is an Angel of Abundance. Take a moment to look at this angel. Do you recognize who is before you? Ask the angel's name. This being is here to guide you along your path of abundance. You begin walking the path with this Angel of Abundance. You may want to take note of your surroundings as you do so. You may hear the tinkling of bells, the plucking of harp strings, the low heartbeat of a drum, or the peaceful lapping of water. Allow your senses to open. Take in all of the blessings around you. Give thanks for them.

Just ahead, you begin to see a blossoming garden. As the path of abundance leads you into the heart of this vibrant garden, you see shafts of sunlight shining through the trees onto the flowers. You feel safe, protected, and peaceful. You see a small crystal-stone circle in the middle of the garden. Your angelic guide prompts you to move forward into the circle. The crystals are small enough to sit on. You may see peridot, pink quartz, amethyst, cinnabar, or jade crystal seats.

Look around and choose your seat. In the center of this circle is a large selenite stone.

You see the stone begin to glow, and before it appear more Angels of Abundance.

Archangel Jophiel, whose name means "the Beauty of God," steps forward and places one hand upon your heart and one hand on the top of your head. Listen now, as she shares a message with you.

Archangel Jophiel steps behind you, as Archangel Michael steps forward to place one hand on your heart and one hand on the top of your head. Listen now to Michael's message.

Archangel Michael steps behind you, as Archangel Raphael steps forward, placing one hand on your heart and one hand on the top of your head. Listen now to Raphael's message.

Archangel Raphael steps behind you, as Archangel Metatron, the angel of the spiritual path, steps forward. He places one hand on your heart and one hand on the top of your head. Listen now to Metatron's message.

Archangel Metatron steps behind you, as Archangel Raziel steps forward. He places one hand on your heart and one hand on the top of your head. Listen now to Raziel's message.

The angels form a circle around you. These Angels of Abundance have attuned and aligned you to your abundance, just as you have asked. Give them thanks for their help, support, and guidance.

You will receive your abundance now, in all areas of your life, in all ways that are for your highest good.

Gently, the light from the Angels of Abundance grows brighter, encasing you in warmth, security, peace, love, and blessings. Know that you can call upon these Angels of Abundance for help at any time.

Breathing in this light, you are ready to bring your awareness back to this time, this place . . . now. On your own time, move your toes and fingers. When you are ready, gently open your eyes.

It's important to be very gentle with yourself after you perform a meditation such as Melissa's. Don't feel that you need to rush off and start a project right away. You haven't wasted any time that must be made up for by working doubly hard for the next few hours. This is work that you deserve and that you owe to yourself. Take time to decompress, relax, and let the messages you have received be absorbed.

ABOUT THE AUTHORS

Doreen Virtue holds BA, MA and PhD degrees in counselling psychology, and is a lifelong clairvoyant who works with the angelic realm. She is the author of *Assertiveness for Earth Angels*, *How to Hear Your Angels* and *The Angel Therapy® Handbook*, among other works. Her products are available in most languages worldwide.

Doreen has appeared on *Oprah*, CNN, *The View*, and other television and radio programmes and she writes regular columns for *Spirit & Destiny* magazines. You can listen to Doreen's live weekly radio show, and call her for a reading, by visiting HayHouseRadio.com®. For more information on Doreen and the workshops she presents, please visit her website.

www.angeltherapy.com

ABOUT THE AUTHORS

Grant Virtue is attending nursing school to obtain his Doctorate of Nursing Practice, while also acting as the technical coordinator for Angel University LLC. A former musician, Grant has studied spirituality throughout his life. In addition to being the author of *Living a Blessed Life*, he is currently working on his first fiction book. Grant lives with his wife, Melissa, and their cat in Florida.

www.grantvirtue.com
Twitter: @grantvirtue

Hay House Titles of Related Interest

YOU CAN HEAL YOUR LIFE, the movie, starring Louise Hay & Friends
(available as a 1-DVD programme and an expanded 2-DVD set)
Watch the trailer at: www.LouiseHayMovie.com

THE SHIFT, the movie,
starring Dr Wayne W. Dyer
(available as a 1-DVD programme and an expanded 2-DVD set)
Watch the trailer at: www.DyerMovie.com

৵৹ ৵৹ ৵৹

THE ABUNDANCE BOOK, by John Randolph Price

HOW TO BECOME A MONEY MAGNET, by Marie-Claire Carlyle

*MIRACLES NOW: 108 Life-Changing Tools for Less Stress, More Flow,
and Finding Your True Purpose,* by Gabrielle Bernstein

THE PROSPEROUS HEART: Creating a Life of 'Enough',
by Julia Cameron with Emma Lively

WISHES FULFILLED: Mastering the Art of Manifesting,
by Dr Wayne W. Dyer

All of the above are available at www.hayhouse.co.uk

৵৹ ৵৹ ৵৹

NOTES